SEVEN DAYS

IN

VIRTUAL

REALITY

Other Books by Jeff Yager

Novels
Atom and Eve (YA)
I Like God
(with Skye Bynes)

Children's books
(illustrated by Nancy Batra)
Chuck and Alfonzo
The Question is Why?

SEVEN DAYS

IN

VIRTUAL

REALITY

A novel

Jeff Yager

Hannacroix Creek Books, Inc.
Stamford, Connecticut

Published by:
Hannacroix Creek Books, Inc.
1127 High Ridge Road, #110
Stamford, CT 06905 USA
https://www.hannacroixcreekbooks.com
e-mail: hannacroix@aol.com
Follow us on Twitter: @hannacroixcreek

ISBN: 978-1-938998-26-3 (trade paperback)

Chapter 1

"Life is like a puzzle with all the corner pieces missing," said the passenger in the back seat. He continued reading his MyFace post out loud. "You just have to go with the flow and be happy with the finished product."

"Right...too bad puzzles suck. With or without all the pieces," said Louis Parker, rolling his eyes. He whipped his 2006 baby blue Masada sedan around the corner of Babylon Lane.

"You don't seem like a normal Ryder driver," the bubbly Millennial passenger told him. "I don't see any bottled water and there's no phone charger. You gotta step it up, Louie."

"Ahh, right...I'm sorry. I forgot it said anywhere that I mustn't disappoint you entitled little—" Louis paused as he stroked his beard.

Then he put the pedal to the floor and sped right through a yellow light turning red, scaring the life out of his passengers.

"You know, I was going to give you two stars...but now I think it will be just one."

The car rolled to a stop. "All right, looks like we're here," said Louis.

"My place is still a few blocks down the road," the customer said, pointing north.

"Yeah, well, if I'm only getting one star, you can walk the rest of the way...plus I can't be late for my other job. So, get the hell out," Louis said as he unlocked the car doors.

"Matter of fact, think I'm going to give you zero stars!" the young man said as he opened the door, got out with his friend, and slammed it shut.

"It is what it is," said Louis. He put the car in reverse and sped around in a U-turn going back the way he came. At the first stop light, he opened his app to find that his total driver rating went down from a 2.9 to a 2.8 rating.

Damn, Louie, you gotta stop pissing off the customers, he said to himself while looking into his own blue eyes in the rear-view mirror.

At the next stop light, Louis looked at his phone to see he had an unread text message from his son, Tommy. The text read, "Dad can I please get the new SB60 Virtual Reality gaming system for my birthday this year? I'll love you forever!"

Louis Parker resided in San Diego, California. At 48, he was still trying to find himself existentially, or as others may call it, he was going through his mid-life crisis. He had two part-time jobs, one as a waiter for a local Italian restaurant, Luigi's, where he had been working for five years. His other job was more of a side gig in his mind, which was driving part-time for Ryder, a new startup rideshare company.

Both jobs seemed to eat away at his soul. Almost as much as his ex-wife, Denise. Their divorce was finalized a year before, and Louis was still adjusting to his new life.

Louis was left with a monthly child support bill for his two children, 15-year-old Tommy and 17-year-old

Natalie, and the couple of hours every other Sunday that he got to spend with them. It was hard for him to get used to the new arrangements.

His wife decided to call it quits roughly two years back after Louis admitted to cheating on her with an escort. They had endured many years of a broken marriage, but they were trying to make it work for the kids even after falling out of love years back, when the kids were still children.

Louis' cheating was not something his wife could look past, and now that their children were both in high school, Denise felt they could handle their parents' divorce. Louis did not put too much effort into keeping things together, either, as he had thought for years that the relationship was crumbling. He stopped caring long enough to make an irreversible mistake that would cost him his marriage, as well as time with his kids.

But he did not know how to cope with the sudden change, even if he knew he was at fault. It was too late, and Denise was already moving on. Louis was starting to miss his family and really beginning to regret his actions and the way he had treated his ex-wife.

Tommy was in his sophomore year, struggling to balance his schoolwork and his videogames. Natalie was in her senior year, getting straight A's on top of her many extracurricular activities. She was the brains of the family and had just gotten accepted into Bacon University where she planned to major in Sociology.

Tommy was preoccupied with videogames and girls but maintained B's and C's on most of his report cards. He was a good kid, but he had started to hang around with the wrong crowd and got in trouble from time to time. He did not have too many good influences in his friend circle.

Louis used to be a fun, wise, optimistic family man. That was before he felt like he had lost almost everything. He was still wise, but far from optimistic or positive. He grew more jaded every day.

Currently, he lived in a one-bedroom apartment on the rough side of town. He stopped seeing his close friends, especially the ones he had made through his wife. Like Jerry, Denise's friend, Mary's husband. They used to watch football games together almost every Sunday for five years.

"GET OUT OF THE WAY, JACKASS!!" Louis shouted at another car in front of him going five miles under the speed limit.

His attention span had never been this short. It was a combination of getting older and realizing he had missed out on many opportunities and dreams that he once had. He moved from job to job for more than twenty years trying to support his family. When the kids were in middle school, Denise became a real estate agent and the real bread winner. Louis did not understand why he still had to pay her alimony and child support when she clearly made much more money than he did.

As he got closer to Luigi's, Louis picked up his phone and looked through his short contact list to find Tommy's number before pressing the call button. The phone rang five times before Tommy picked up. "What's up, Dad?" he asked.

"Just checking in to see how you are. I missed ya," Louis said.

"I'm good. Just playing Wars of the Goddesses, you know. Killing it and shit," said Tommy. "Umm, how have you been?"

"Same, you know. Living the dream," said Louis as he hit his blinker before making a right onto Spruce Street.

"You always say that Dad," said Tommy. "Everything okay?"

"Of course. I'm as cool as a cucumber...you know that," said Louis.

"The coolest," said Tommy in a sarcastic tone before laughing.

"Listen, I got your text about the virtual game thing you wanted. I'm going to see what I can do. But hey, son. I was thinking...maybe I can take you and your sister out to eat tomorrow night or something. I don't know, just missed seeing you guys. I know it's not Sunday, but I just wanted to hang out a bit more," said Louis.

"Yeah, sure. Maybe. I gotta ask Mom, but I don't see why not. Maybe we can go get pizza or something. Sorry, I'm kind of distracted at the moment. I'm in the process of getting my ass kicked in this damn game right now," Tommy responded.

"How you been doing in school?" asked Louis.

"Not too bad. Got a math exam tomorrow."

"Oh yeah? Did you study?"

"Not really."

"Well, that's going to be a problem. Get it? Like a math problem?" said Louis.

"I get it, Dad. I'll study tonight. And your jokes are still awful."

"Don't lie. You love them. Anyways…I'll you're your Mom and mention it too, but let me know what she says," said Louis.

"Will do. Gotta go, Dad. I love ya."

"Love you too, son," said Louis as he ran a red light at the last second since he was already going to be a couple minutes late for his shift. They both hung up as Louis turned up the volume on his radio and started to drive faster.

Louis arrived at Luigi's for his night shift. He was barely able to change into his uniform before walking through the door. The restaurant was busy, and Louis was already exhausted from his second job.

"Louie!" shouted Greg. Greg managed Luigi's. He always had a look on his face like he just stepped on a toy. While he liked him overall, Louis thought that his boss was angry at heart and loved taking it out on his employees.

"Yeah, what is it, Greg? That blonde never called you back from the bar last week?" said Louis as he started laughing.

"Louie, we've been getting complaints that you have been driving for Ryder on your way back from work. What's up with that? Don't we pay you enough here?"

Louis clocked into the computer above the register before grabbing a bread stick from a basket and taking a bite.

"No...you don't pay me enough. And I didn't think it was a crime to have a side job, either" he said.

"It's not. But when you give our customers rides home when you clock out, then there may be a problem. I think management is getting pretty pissed about it, to be honest."

"Uhhh, you're the manager, Greg."

"Yeah and frankly I think it's stupid as hell, Lou."

"Well, Mr. Pucci was quite hammered that night. I figured he could use a ride. I was just doing a nice thing."

"And did you turn on that silly app while you did your good deed for the year?" asked Greg.

"You weren't gonna pay me for it, so yeah. Screw it. Sorry, not sorry, Greg…I think that's what my daughter says. Yeah. Sorry, not sorry," Louis said.

"Next time it's your last time doing that crap because I'll have to fire you. You know that, Louie," Greg exclaimed.

"Yeah, yeah…I got it. Now can I get to work, boss?" asked Louis sarcastically.

"Watch that attitude, Louie. I mean it."

Louis put on his name tag, looked at Greg and said, "Hey Greg."

"Yeah, Lou?"

"Have you ever felt like… if only we could get a do-over? Like if only I could change so many dumb decisions and mistakes I've made in the past."

"Wow. Sounds like somebody has a lot on his mind. Lou, we all feel that way sometimes. But you gotta live in the present. That's what's important. You can't change the past, Louie. You gotta accept it. Plus, I'm not doing too bad for myself anyway. I'm happy with where I am," said Greg.

"You're an alcoholic with a gambling problem," said Louis.

"Maybe, but I still make more money than you do and I'm more handsome, so shut your trap, Louis, and get to work! Time is money!"

Chapter 2

The next week, Louis sat at his favorite Italian restaurant with a beautiful 30-something woman. Her long brown hair flowed down to her shiny black dress. She looked over at Louis from across the table and smiled.

Louis was having a hard time getting back into the dating scene. He was not actively trying to meet someone. But once he saw that his ex-wife had a new boyfriend, he had to try to get his mind off of her. And it was not like riding a bike at all for Louis. He was trying to relearn how to talk to women and it was all brand new to him again. He was with his wife for nearly twenty years. He forgot how to go on a date. But the new freedom he had gained after the divorce was finalized gave him all of the motivation that he needed to give dating a shot.

"So…Tina. Where did you grow up?" Louis asked.

"Well, my family moved around a bunch. But we spent a lot of time in Buffalo, New York. As well as a couple years in Pennsylvania, and Colorado for a year, back when I was in high school," Tina explained as she took a sip of her glass of Pinot Grigio.

"That's great. Remarkably interesting," said Louis as he looked over at the clock on the wall of the restaurant/bar. He was set up on a blind date by his friend, Tim. He was reluctant to show up but decided to in the end.

"So, how do you know Suzy and Timothy?" she asked.

"Me and Tim worked together a few years ago. Our kids are nearly the same age. He's a good guy," said Louis.

"Oh, cool, cool," said his date. "Suzy and I do yoga together. She's a sweetheart."

"Yeah. I like Suzy. Pretty cool gal," said Louis as he took a sip from his bottle of beer.

"How about you? Tell me about your family, growing up, whatever you want...you seem like an interesting man, Louis," she said.

"Sure, Tina. Let's see...my kids are great. Rather not talk about the wife...I mean...ex-wife right now." He drank his beer as he began to shake subtly out of nervousness.

"Okay. I understand that. You and your kids close?" Tina asked.

"Yeah, I mean, I think so…I don't know, every year it's different. But yeah. I like to think we are. I love the hell out of them, ya know?"

"I don't have kids myself, so I can only imagine. Maybe one day. So, what was it like growing up?" she asked as she picked up her glass of wine.

"Oh boy. That's a lot to unload on you right now, hon."

"No, go on. I'd love to hear it. I can see it in your eyes. You've lived a wild life. I can tell. You've seen some things," she said.

He got more nervous as the conversation went on, and he finally decided to let his guard down a bit.

"Well, I guess every family can be a little dysfunctional sometimes, right?"

"Of course," she said.

"Well, mine was no different. We were an odd family, at least it seemed to me that we were."

"Whose isn't?" she said. "My parents disowned me for a few years after college," said Tina.

"Well, you ever watch those movies that you don't really understand, yet you can't get enough of, or you just can't stop watching?" asked Louis.

"Yeah. I think so," said Tina.

"That's my family. We were chaotic. We were cruel to each other, but we always loved each other. My parents were hard on us because they knew the world was hard. My brothers, sister, and I fought all the time. But in the end, I think it made us tougher, or something. I don't know," said Louis.

He started to think back on his childhood and almost went into a trance as flashbacks circumnavigated his mind.

Then Tina reached over the table and tapped him on the shoulder.

"Hello? You were talking and then just went off into the clouds on me," she said.

The waiter brought their food and placed it on the table. "You two enjoy," he said.

"I'm sorry," said Louis. "I guess mentioning my family brought me back a little bit. My bad."

"It's all good," said his date as she smelled her plate. "Looks so delicious!"

"Yeah, sure does," said Louis as he took a sip of his beer and began to cut into his veal parmigiana.

"So, a little off subject. Do you believe in God? Heaven, hell, all that?" she asked as she bit into her glazed salmon.

"Well, you know, I guess I do. But, haven't had a good conversation with the Big Guy in a long time, you could say," Louis said as he cut his main course into smaller pieces and drank the rest of his beer. "Waiter," he said as their server walked by. "Can I get another one of these bad boys?"

"Coming right up."

"So, yeah, I guess…sure. And lately, I feel like I've been going through hell, so I pray to God there is a heaven after this, at least, you know? Or something like that, I suppose."

"Wow," she said. "I know exactly what you mean."

"So how 'bout you?" he asked.

The server walked an ice-cold bottle of his favorite beer, a seasonal lager made locally by Briscoe Brewery downtown.

"Short answer to those questions is yes. But if you asked me back when I was with my shitty abusive ex, Phil, then I may have said no," Tina explained.

"Oh, I'm sorry to hear that," said Louis as he took a sip of his beer.

"Don't be. I'm better off now. He was a lesson I guess I was supposed to learn," she said. "Or something like that. I don't know, but if there is a God, he certainly works in mysterious ways, that's for sure."

"Amen to that," said Louis.

After dinner, the two made their way out of the restaurant and onto the sidewalk where Louis reached into his pocket and pulled out his pack of cigarettes. "Mind if I get a drag of that?" Tina asked.

"Of course not. Would you like your own?" Louis asked.

"No, just a couple of drags is fine. I've been good lately. Trying to quit…but that wine is telling me to take a puff or two," said Tina.

Louis sparked up his cigarette and took a couple puffs before passing it to her. After two long drags, Tina gave it back to Louis. "Okay, that's good. No more for me," she said.

He continued smoking as Louis grabbed Tina's hand and they started to walk down the street. He had parked a few blocks away and was not sure if she wanted the night to continue or not. So, they just walked and talked. They were both a little bit buzzed, but Louis only had two drinks, while Tina seemed a bit more inebriated after a few tall glasses of red wine.

They walked by a bar that had a live band playing and Tina insisted they stop in and listen to a few songs. Louis went along with it, mostly because he had not been on a date in months and he did not want to ruin it.

After the band covered several big hits from the 80s and 90s, Louis stifled a yawn. He had worked all day, and he was now stuffed after a big Italian dinner.

Tina was dancing and trying to have a good time, so Louis rallied on. She reminded him of his ex-wife when they first met. She would always force him to go to concerts he did not care to see and made him dance with her even when he rarely ever enjoyed dancing.

At the bar, Louis tried to get the bartender's attention so he could get a drink for his date.

There was a long line of people waiting, so Louis just rolled his eyes and looked at the time on his phone as it got later and later.

"Over here!" he yelled to the bartender who was flirting with a couple of customers and taking his sweet time. The bartender put up a finger and said, "One second! Be with you when I can!"

"Ugh," said Louis as he looked over at Tina who was just enjoying the music. He let out another yawn.

"Whoa, Louie?" said a man next to him at the bar.

"Oh shit. Jack Johansen, right?" said Louis.

"Yeah, dude. How the hell are you?" the man asked.

"I'm just…you know…living the dream."

"For sure, for sure. Same, dude," said Jack as he took a shot of whiskey and looked around the club like he was being followed.

"How about you?" asked Louis as he was still a bit fuzzy on how he even knew the man in the first place. He could not put his finger on it, but he knew that they had met before.

"I'm living my best life, Bro," said Jack.

"That's great to hear, man," said Louis as he tried to get the bartender's attention again. No luck. He looked back at the man as he tried to think where he knew him from.

"How is Roy?" asked Jack.

"Wait, what?" said Louis.

"Roy, you know, your brother?" said Jack. Then Louis remembered. Growing up, Jack was close friends with Roy. They may have even lived together at one time.

Roy was Louis' younger brother by seven years. They were close growing up, but after a couple of bad fights over the years, they grew apart and barely spoke.

"Yeah, last I heard, Roy was up in Los Angeles, doing it hella big."

"Well, not so sure, to be quite honest with you. My brother and I don't really talk these days," said Louis as he waved over at the bartender again.

"Oh, that sucks to hear. Well, I'm sure he would love it if you reached out to him sometime. If I remember correctly, he always looked up to you and shit," said Jack as he took another shot of whiskey.

"I doubt that," said Louis.

"Well, he always said that once you started your family, you forgot about the one you already had. Or something along those lines."

"Really? He said that?" asked Louis.

"Yeah, I mean I'm not trying to stir up anything or nothing. But I think I remember that faintly," said Jack.

"Nah, it's cool. I mean, he was right. I didn't visit as much as I could have."

"Well, it's never too late, ya know? You can't let the past control you, Louie," said Jack as he put his arm around Louis and gave his shoulder a pat. Jack was the second person to give him advice about the past that week. Jack reeked of liquor from his breath and pores as the alcohol fermented in his sweat.

21

"You might be right," said Louis as the bartender finally came over to him. "Yeah, hey, can I get a…what'd she call it? A 'sex in the beach'?"

"You mean a 'sex on the beach'?" asked the bartender as he looked over at some ladies and winked at them.

"Yeah, that, and whatever beer you have on tap," said Louis.

"Sure thing, sir," said the bartender as he started to make the drinks.

"Louie, I must say, you've always been such an interesting character to me," said Jack, who began to slur his words.

"Is that so?"

"For sure, dude. Like, I would love to pick your brain some time, it's like…I bet you see life totally different being from like a generation before your brother and me and shit," said Jack before he stumbled a little.

"Right," said Louis. He gave the bartender twenty bucks for the drinks, then stepped away from the bar.

"Well, listen. I gotta get back to my friends, but if you ever wanna link up, here's my card," said Jack as he looked through his torn-up wallet to find his business card. He handed it to Louis. "This is my last business card. I think it's a sign. That it's meant for you."

Louis looked at the card:

Jack Johansen
CEO/Developer
Mindtrick Games Inc.

It also had his phone number and office address listed on the card.

"Neat," said Louis at he looked at Jack. "So, what, you're into videogames or something?"

"Actually, yes. How could you tell?" asked Jack.

"It says Mindtrick Games," said Louis. He looked at the time on his phone and it read 11:49. He let out another yawn.

"Well, you know there are all sorts of games, not just videogames, right? Like shit.... Life is a game if you really think about it," said Jack.

"It says CEO, like what, you founded it or something?"

"Yeah, you can say that. Or maybe, it found me, hah-hah."

"Right."

"No, yeah. I created it with my buddy Will three years ago. We develop games and new algorithms for games. Specifically, virtual reality games. You know because that's what's in these days, and that is our future," said Jack.

"Yeah. My son Tommy has been asking for one of them VR console thingamajigs for years now."

"Nice. I don't blame him. The tech is awesome. You know, I may be able to hook you and your son up with one of our latest consoles," said Jack.

"Wow, you don't have to do that, man. Really. But this is so cool. Awesome to see how good you're doing. Congrats, really."

"Thanks, my man. We're working on a new game right now that…fingers crossed…is going to change the entire world, Louie."

"I don't doubt that one bit," said Louis. "You've always been into trying to change the world or whatever from what I can remember."

"Oh, hell yeah. Listen, it's been great catching up. You have my card. Shit, if you're ever looking for a new job, or just want to get a coffee or something, hit me up. It's on me. I'll be expecting a call from you, my old friend. I mean, my longtime friend, you're far from old, my dude."

"Nah, you're right. Old works," said Louis before laughing.

"Shut the hell up. What are you like thirty-eight, thirty-nine?" asked Jack, half-jokingly.

"Sure, that sounds good, yep, thirty-eight."

"You don't even look it," said Jack as he shook his hand.

"You're too kind," said Louis. "I'll give you a ring sometime. Later, Jack. It was great running into you," he said as he waved goodbye.

"Later, my old friend," said Jack as he meandered to the other side of the bar.

Louis returned to his date. Tina was dancing to one of her favorite songs, "Smoke in the Air," by one of her top five bands of all time, The Swingers.

"What took you so long?" she asked Louis.

"Sorry about that. Ran into somebody I haven't seen in forever," he said as he handed her the mixed drink.

"Yum, that looks tasty," she said as she took a sip from her straw. "Dance with me!"

Louis looked at the business card that Jack gave him one more time before putting it in his wallet. "Sure. Why not?" he said before joining her on the dance floor. Then Louis started rocking back and forth as a mixture of exhaustion and excitement consumed him.

Chapter 3

The next morning, Louis left Tina's apartment and started his day by logging into the Ryder app to see if anyone close-by needed a ride. He wanted to compensate for the money he had spent on dinner and drinks the night before. He had no regrets about staying with Tina except for wanting to get out of her place as soon as he could. He would have gone back to his own apartment and passed out much earlier if she had not convinced him to stay over.

He picked up his first passenger who was a college girl that needed a ride twenty miles out of town.

After that, Louis took six rides before deciding to go back to the apartment he rented on a month-to-month basis. He wanted to brush his teeth and take a quick nap before starting his shift at his second job at the restaurant.

Louis sat on his bed and turned on the television. He started watching one of his favorite crime shows as he drifted off into a deep sleep.

When he woke up, the TV was showing a commercial for a new virtual reality game that at the end read, "Made by Mindtrick Games." The graphics looked so real that Louis could not even tell it was a videogame.

Louis looked outside and saw it was starting to get dark. He began to panic as he searched for his phone before finding it in his pants pocket. He looked at the time and realized he had slept through the alarm and now he was an hour late for his shift at Luigi's.

"Shit!" he said as he threw on his pants, grabbed his car keys and wallet, and ran outside to his car. He quickly started the car, and sped the entire way to his job, roughly four miles from his apartment.

Louis parked in the employee parking lot, locked his car doors, and ran through the back door.

He found his manager, Greg, and immediately apologized. "I'm sorry I'm late…my alarm never went off."

"Save it, Louie," said Greg as he ran around during the dinner rush, losing his mind. "Look, Margarette came in and covered for you, so you're off the hook. You can go back to whatever it is you were doing that was more important than your job, Louie."

"What? Greg, I'm here. I'm ready to work."

"Well, it's too late, bud. I'm sorry but, I gotta let you go. This is your third strike. I'm sorry but you're fired."

"You know what? Screw you," said Louis, as he grabbed a slice of pizza out of a box that the cashier was about to give to a customer.

"Screw this place," he said as he took a bite into the slice. "Oh, and by the way, this pizza sucks! Inauthentic trash. There's three better spots down the block alone!"

Louis walked out the back door and slammed it shut as he headed to his car.

"Shit!" he yelled as he unlocked, opened the door, got in, and slammed it shut. Then Louis skidded out of the parking lot, sticking up his middle finger out of the window.

"Damn it," he said as he logged into the app and waited for riders. "So much for two jobs, huh?" he muttered as he turned up the volume on the radio and cruised down the road. He tried to act like losing his main job did not faze him. He tried to forget he'd even worked at Luigi's. He hated that place. Now he just had to figure out how to come up with more substantial income to replace it.

After getting only a couple of riders over the next two hours, Louis pulled into a gas station and parked on the side.

He got out, leaned up against his sedan and sparked up a cigarette. He tried his hardest not to smoke in the car, so every now and then he would pull over and have one or two. For some reason, he was not getting many riders. It could have been because of his rating getting progressively worse.

"What the hell am I gonna do?" he asked himself. Then he looked in his wallet and pulled out the business card from Jack.

He looked at the card for a while before taking out his phone and going through his contacts. He scrolled down to his brother Roy, whom he had not spoken to in an awfully long time. He was not even sure if it was still his number. He pushed the call button and the phone started to ring.

"Louis?" Roy answered.

"Roy, it's been a while. How the hell are you?"

"Whoa, this is a surprise. How you been?" asked his brother.

"Hanging in there, I suppose," said Louis.

"Same, man, same. What's it been? A year since we talked?" asked Roy.

"More like two, I think," said Louis.

"Good to hear from you," said Roy.

Louis took a drag from his cigarette before flicking the butt into the street. "Likewise," he said. "How's LA been treating you?"

"Well, shit's been rough lately. But you know, here in LA, every day is a new day. Work has been…decent, I guess," said his brother.

"I bet," said Louis as he sparked up another cigarette. "Listen, so, I ran into your old pal, Jack Johansen, at a bar…we talked for a bit."

"Wow, really? I haven't spoken to that lunatic in ages."

"Yeah, I was wondering, what's his deal?" asked Louis.

"What do you mean?"

"Well, I was thinking about giving him a call. He spoke about a possible job when I saw him, and…"

Roy interrupted, "What is it? Something to do with Mindtrick or something?"

"Well, yeah, I'd assume so. We didn't discuss it, but he mentioned if I'm looking for work, yada-yada."

"Jack is surprisingly good people. I mean, he hasn't screwed me over too much. But that doesn't mean I would trust him with my life either, you know what I'm saying?

"No, not really. Enlighten me," said Louis.

"Look, he's a good guy, but the dude used to do heavy drugs. He was really spontaneous…I mean, he's just sort of…reckless. Absolute tech wiz, but reckless. He was always a good friend, but I'm not too sure I would work for him. That's not me telling you what to do, just my opinion."

"He might have been a little bit drunk when I saw him, but he didn't seem to be high or on drugs or anything."

"Well, I don't know. Maybe he's clean now. It's been a while since we've hung out," Roy explained.

"Money's been really tight, and if this is legit, maybe I should go for it," said Louis as he inhaled the smoke from his cigarette.

"If you want to go for it, go for it," said Roy. "I've never worked with the guy, but I do know his games are brilliant. He's always talking about changing the world. Sometimes it even gave me the creeps. But then again, everyone is creepy to me if I'm around them too much."

"Hah, right, so, maybe I'll give him a call. Was just checking to make sure there weren't any major red flags I should know about," said Louis.

"Bro, it sounds like you already made up your mind. So just do it."

"All right. Thanks Roy," said Louis.

Anytime. Oh, and Lou. Next time let's not make it two years before we talk again."

"I agree," said Louis.

"And San Diego isn't that far from LA, if you know what I mean, big brother."

"Yeah, I get it," said Louis. "Look, I gotta run. Be safe out in LA, Bro."

"Will do, Louie," said Roy as he ended the call.

Louis was sitting at his tiny kitchen table with his kids who were busy on their cell phones. His daughter was taking selfies and his son was playing a mobile game on his phone. He did not mind, as he was simply happy to have them over to spend some time with him, whether they gave him their attention or not.

He was waiting on a call back from Jack about a possible interview for whatever job Jack thought would be a good fit. Jack's receptionist had said Jack would call Louis at his earliest convenience.

That was three days ago. Louis was starting to give up on the idea and now was scrolling online for job openings in the area. He found a couple of decent jobs he thought looked promising, but he had no clue whether most were legitimate. He'd applied for two warehouse positions outside of San Diego, as well as one at a car lot where his poker buddy said he would try to put in a good word for him.

"How's school going?" Louis asked his kids.

Neither one of them answered, as they were too distracted to hear him. Louis cleared his throat.

"So! How has school been going?" he asked again, louder than before.

"Whoa, it's fine," said Tommy.

"What the hell, Dad?" asked Natalie.

"What? I can't ask you guys about school anymore. Geesh," said Louis as he took a bite from the cheeseburger he'd cooked on the grill. "By the way, your food is gonna get cold if you don't eat it."

"School's fine, Dad, but you already know that," said his daughter as she continued to scroll through pictures on her favorite social media app, ScreenTap. Then she took a small bite from her burger and, "The burger's fine, Dad. Like all of your burgers. They're good, okay?"

"Yikes," said Louis as he looked over at Tommy. Tommy then took a big bite into his cheeseburger.

"Wow. This is actually awesome, Dad."

"Thanks. I can make a good meal here and there, you know. Your mother just hogged the kitchen most of the time. But I tell you what. Your Dad can make a mean chicken pot pie," he said as he took another bite. They continued to be distracted by their phones. "But don't worry. I'll make yours without the pot," Louis said.

Tommy just rolled his eyes at another one of his father's attempts at a joke.

"That's great, Dad," said his daughter who double-tapped on a picture of her friend at the beach.

"You kids and your damn phones. You know one day I'll be gone, right? You should appreciate me now while I'm still here," Louis said.

"Dad, we do appreciate you. Mom just doesn't let us use our phones at dinner, and you do…so we're just enjoying the moment, you know?" said Tommy as he lost another round of BombRockets, the free, yet addictive mobile app he and all of his friends had been playing for the last month.

"Didn't think of that," said their father.

"Yeah, Dad. You know we love you," said Natalie as she stared at her phone, waiting for likes to come in for the latest selfie she just posted. She added a black and white filter to it and captioned it "Dinner at Dad's" with the hashtags #selfie, #sandiegogirl, and #girlgenius. She always put random hashtags on her posts. She had three hundred and twenty-three followers and she followed thousands of people. She could never understand how other girls at school could get so many likes and followers. She did not know what she was doing wrong.

Then Louis' phone started vibrating. It looked like the number from the business card, so he answered it.

"This is Louie," he said before taking a deep breath. He got up and went into the bathroom of his small apartment so he could hear better.

"Louie!" Jack shouted through the phone. "Sorry it took so long for me to return your call. We've had a busy couple of days finishing this new beta for a game we're getting ready to test out. This one…this one is really going to change the world, Louie."

"Sound's great," said Louis.

Jack responded, "So how can I help you? Is this a coffee call or a job call? Business or pleasure? What's up?"

"Well, to be honest, Jack, it is about a job. I recently came into some unfortunate circumstances this week, and…"

Jack cut him off.

"Save it, my dude. You don't have to explain yourself to me. Or to anyone, for that matter," he said.

"Cool, thanks, I mean…cool, you're right."

"So, you need a job, Louie?" asked Jack.

"I do, man, I really do. Bills piling up, this, that, everything seems to be happening at once. Anything you got to offer, I'm willing to take it I mean entertain it," Louis replied.

"You know, a temporary position did recently open up, actually," said Jack.

"Oh wow, perfect," said Louis. "What job, if you don't mind me asking?"

"Well, I mean, I guess you'd be sort of like, a tester. For a new product...a virtual reality game we have practically just finished. I think you may be the perfect candidate for the job. You seem like the right guy," said Jack.

"Jack, listen. I really appreciate it, whatever you need, I'm your guy," said Louis, jumping for joy in his bathroom. He nearly smacked his head on the ceiling, which was only two feet higher than he was. "Thank you, brother."

"Don't sweat it, my guy. Listen. Why don't you come in on Monday, let's say around nine o'clock, and we'll do a formal interview with my partners. If all goes well, you can start that day if you like."

"That works for me," said Louis.

"All right, this will be great. Can't wait. I gotta run. See you Monday, Louie."

"See ya then," he responded before the call ended.

"Yes!" Louis shouted as he left his bathroom and went back to the kitchen table.

Louis sat down with his kids. "Guess what?" he asked as they both looked up from their phones.

"What?" they said at the same time.

"Your father may have just landed a new job," he said.

"Awesome, Dad. Thought you had a few already, though," said Tommy as he went back to playing his game.

"Well, I sorta just lost my main job, and driving hasn't been paying enough to get by. So, I needed something new. And guess what, Tommy? It's a job working for this videogame company called Mindtrick."

"Shut the front door, what?"

"Yeah, I recently ran into an old friend of your Uncle Roy's. One thing led to another, and now I guess I may be working for him, or them. Whatever. Not exactly sure, but I think it may have something to do with virtual reality."

"No freaking way. You? Of all people? That's crazy, Dad. I mean…congratulations," said Tommy.

"Thanks, son," said Louis as he finished his cheeseburger. "Guess they're gonna have to teach this old dog some new tricks, huh?" he said as he laughed and brought his plate to the sink. His smile covered his face from cheek to cheek. He was excited. Things were starting to finally go his way. Everything was coming up Louie.

Chapter 4

Monday morning came and Louis was already awake for hours. He was getting ready for his interview at nine with Jack.

He trimmed his beard, showered, brushed his teeth, and donned his favorite button-down shirt and khakis.

After he locked his door, he made his way down the three flights of stairs and out to his car in the apartment building parking lot.

He lit up a cigarette as he got close to his car. He took four puffs before throwing it on the ground and stomping it. *What am I thinking? Can't smell like cigarettes during this interview*, he said to himself as he unlocked his car and got in.

He pulled up to the big shiny silver building downtown and parked across the street in the only open parking space he could find. Louis put a few quarters into the meter, which gave him two hours of parking. He still had fifteen minutes until his interview, so he played on his phone for a bit.

He checked the rideshare app to find his driver rating had gone down one more point. Louis held the app's button and then deleted it altogether. He thought it would give him added confidence for the interview; that he was all in.

This had to work. He felt like he had nothing else going for him, and no better options coming his way either.

Louis walked into the lobby and looked on the wall to see the big Mindtrick logo. He walked over to the receptionist and signed in on the check-in clipboard on the front desk. "We'll call you when Mr. Johansen is ready to see you," said the girl.

"Sounds good," said Louis as he took a seat and waited.

A few minutes went by and it was nine o'clock. Jack walked out to greet Louis in the lobby. "There's my guy!" he yelled as he walked over to shake Louis' hand.

"Glad you found the place," he said. "Follow me to my office. That's where we can do the interview, Lou. Hey, that rhymes," he said.

"Sure does. And glad to be here," said Louis. "This building is incredible, by the way."

"That's nice of you to say," said Jack.

Louis looked around as Jack led him down the long hallway past all sorts of interesting looking rooms. Some people were working in offices, while others lounged in the break rooms or played different videogames in futuristic round chairs that hovered above the ground. Virtual reality headsets, bodysuits, and other technology that Louis had never seen before were arranged in at least ten different rooms, with many people running around like they all had a deadline to make. The place felt different than anywhere Louis had been before. It was an unreal sight for him to witness. Bright white lights lit up the spacious office building with a blue tint.

"My son would love this stuff," said Louis.

"Hopefully, all of his friends will too," Jack responded before laughing.

"They will. Trust me," Louis exclaimed.

He looked around in awe at the wondrous things he could not even have imagined before seeing them with his own eyes.

"And here we are. Take a seat right by my desk and we'll get started," said Jack as he opened the door to his office. The sign on the door read, "Mr. Jack."

Louis took a seat and noticed a computer in the corner that displayed four men on a video chat call. "I thought you said we'd be meeting with your partners," Louis said as he tried to take it all in. He took a deep breath and began to sweat.

"Oh, we are. These are my partners. Three in Tokyo, and my co-founder, Will, is in Arkansas. Will's mostly a silent partner, these days. We do most of our meetings through video chat."

"No problem. Just all very new to me. That's all."

"Many things here will be new to you, Lou," said Jack as he took a seat behind his desk. "Don't worry about those guys. They're only here because it's a part of our policy. If it were up to me, it would be just you and I, my friend. But you know, we gotta accommodate corporate, you know what I'm saying?"

"No, I get it." Louis responded.

"Don't worry. They don't really speak most of the time, so it will be virtually just us, pun intended."

Louis laughed nervously, "Cool, cool," he said.

"So, let's get started, shall we?"

"Let's do it," said Louis.

"Look. We don't have to make this some in-depth psychiatric assessment or anything. I know you're good people. I mean your brother was one of my best friends. I trust you. That's not what I'm worried about. What I'm worried about is if you can handle the workload, and experience overall…here at Mindtrick."

"Well, sure this is all new to me, but I learn very quickly anywhere I go. That won't be any different here. You tell me what I need to do, and I'll do it to the best of my ability. That's my word," explained Louis.

"Awesome to hear, Louie," said Jack as he drank his coffee and looked over to the men on the computer screen. He nodded and continued, "So, if that's the case, you may be just the man we've been looking for. You have the opportunity to help us change the world of videogames, and then, ultimately, the world in general."

"Then, well...there is no doubt in my mind that I am your guy," said Louis. "Whatever you need, we'll make it happen. I'm a company man."

Jack smiled. "Where to begin? There's so much to say, and we don't have all the time in the world. Now that I think about it, no one does. Wonder where that phrase even came from?" Jack started to get off topic.

"Who knows?" asked Louis who was doing his best to smile during the interview and trying his hardest to make Jack like him. At least like him enough to turn a temporary position into a possible full-time career that would make his son proud. Something they could bond over.

He still could not believe he landed this interview, which was going well so far. Louis looked out of the window of Jack's office in awe at the view he was witnessing. The clouds and the buildings blended like a portrait. *This is the real American Dream right here*, he thought to himself.

"It's truly something, isn't it?" asked Jack as he saw Louis looking out the window.

"Sure is," Louis responded.

"When we bumped into each other that night at the bar, I don't know what it was, but something told me you and I would be seeing much more of each other. I had no clue that meant working together. Which is awesome, by the way. I just had a feeling, though. It's crazy. That happens from time to time," said Jack.

Louis tried not to get distracted by all the technology that surrounded him. It was utterly fascinating. But he kept his eyes on Jack and focused on the interview at hand. He tried not to get too far ahead of himself.

Louis played along, "I think I had that same feeling, Mr. Jack," he said before laughing. After a short pause, Jack started to laugh as well.

"Very funny," Jack said as he finished his coffee. "Damn, that's good." He placed his mug on his desk.

"Jack, if you don't mind me asking…what is the position?" asked

Louis grew more nervous as the interview went on. He was not sure if the guy was full of it or not. It also felt way too good to be true. But either way, it was all impressive.

"I'm getting there, buddy, relax. It takes a bit of explaining, especially if you're not an avid gamer like most of the others that held this type of position before you. Which was the main reason I thought you could be great for this.

"Listen, to be completely blunt with you, Jack... I don't know the first thing about virtual reality or any of this new videogame stuff. I barely even know how to work my smartphone," said Louis.

"That's funny. Barely even know how to use your phone, hilarious. And you know what, Louie? That is why you're perfect for this," said Jack.

"So, what exactly is 'this'?" asked Louis.

"Okay, well. First, we have this new game we've developed that is...well, next level. Some may even say next-next level."

"Right. So, what are we talking about?"

"Well. Right now, this is entirely experimental. If all goes well with our trial run, we will release it to the public for sale in the somewhat near future," Jack explained. "We've been developing this game for years, and we're finally ready to test it."

"I see," said Louis.

"We have game designers that went to school to become quantum physicists. These games are a work of science more than anything. We are going to push forward and advance videogames, virtual reality, science, and life as we know it. This game is going to win me the Nobel Peace Prize. Just watch." said Jack.

"And you think I'm the right guy for this?" asked Louis.

"You know what? Let me show you around." Jack stood up and said to the video chat, "I'm going to give Louie a little tour of the facility, if that's all right with you guys."

The men all nodded as Jack walked out the door. Louis stood up and followed him closely.

"Nice, a little time alone for us to talk man-to-man. Finally. I always feel so weird with them staring at me during interviews and meetings all the time. Like, lemme get some space, am I right?" asked Jack.

First thing that came to Louis' head was why Jack wanted to talk in private at all. It was a bit odd, but he tried not to make too much out of it.

They walked by an intern and Jack handed him his red and black coffee cup, "Fill this up for me, thanks."

"Yes sir, Mr. Jack," said the intern, and he ran down the hallway.

"Now, where the hell was I?" said Jack as they started to walk around the building. Louis caught a glimpse of what looked like a man with a VR headset of some sort and what appeared to be bionic arms. "Oh, that's right, the job," said Jack after his brief brain fart.

"Right, the job," Louis responded as they continued walking around the building.

"It's a bit much to take in all at once, but I'll try to explain it in a way you'll understand, as much as possible, you know. Stop me if I lose you at any time, Louie," said Jack.

"No problem," said Louis.

"I'm going to assume you aren't that familiar with our past VR products, correct?"

"That's fair to say," said Louis as he looked around at all the astonishing technology. "I was never really that much of a gamer or whatever, but I always wanted to get into it. Just never got the time."

"That is totally cool, Lou," said Jack.

The intern then ran up to them trying not to spill the hot coffee.

"Thanks, Mark," Jack said as he took his coffee cup and continued walking.

"I know you guys work with virtual reality, among other things, but I would probably mispronounce the names of your games if I tried."

"Hah, that's funny, Louie. Well, our biggest seller to date is 'Crash Course 3', which is a virtual reality racing game. That is our number one money-maker. But we also dabble in other genres of games. We have developed algorithms so unique that we can't even use most of them and end up selling the patents to other companies that can use the tech. Over the past two years, however, we have been developing this new game, something I came up with out of nowhere. It uses first-of-its-kind technology, and we are awfully close to our initial test trial run. Should be just a week or so until the final safety protocols are in place," Jack explained.

"Neat. Very cool," said Louis.

"You still with me, my man? Anyway, our new game isn't just virtual reality, but rather virtual, simulated, and augmented reality, all combined into one electrifying experience. I like to think of it as 'Interactive Reality' technology. Still trying to get everyone else on board with calling it that. Anyhow, we have been developing this bad boy for practically two years now, and I must say, I think I reinvented the wheel here, Louie. We have figured out how to integrate computed quantum mechanics into our virtual algorithm. It is quite hard to comprehend at first, well, actually most folks never fully grasp it. But it works, and we have ventured into a world that hasn't been born yet," said Jack as he took a sip from his hot coffee.

"Sounds crazy," said Louis.

"Yes, it is. Quite crazy. This game, this technology, has never existed before. If I hadn't developed this monumental and innovative algorithm, it never would have existed at all. Thank god it came to me one night, almost in a dream. Except I was awake. But the idea just came to me like a download to my brain from some sort of extraterrestrial being in the sky, and we just ran with it. Now we have a beta ready to test for any bugs that may be hidden in the system. If all goes well, we're looking at putting it out on the market within a year, two at tops."

"I do not doubt that in the slightest," said Louis.

"Good. That's good. I've had enough doubters already. I know you're on my side, Louie. I always liked you, and I am starting to really think you might be the one for the job."

"Wow, I mean, it would be my honor, Jack."

"Oh yeah, so the game. Well. It is called *Seven Days VR*. It was actually called *Seven Days in Virtual Reality* at first, but it was too long, so I decided to just shorten it to *Seven Days VR*."

"Sounds cool," Louis said as he grew more and more curious as to what his new position entailed.

"Oh, it is cool. Basically, it is a brand-new virtual reality experience, so to speak. The objective of the game is simple. The player picks seven days from his or her own past that he or she gets to relive… through…virtual reality of course."

The look on Louis' face changed from confused to shocked as he said, "I'm not exactly sure if I understand, Jack. How would that even work?"

"Exactly what I said. In *Seven Days VR*, you, the user, get to relive seven days of your past. Your very own past. Your own memories. With recent discoveries in technology, we have come up with ways to connect the game's system to your brain using our next-gen VR system. We use neurotechnology that syncs up with the console, and within an hour of updates, the system can access any memory from the past that the player desires to relive. Then, with our quantum physics realm code, we are able to transfer you to your past by way of the electrons within your memories alone. I know it's a lot to take in all at once, but that is the best way I can explain it. You'll start to figure more out as time goes on. I wish I were in your shoes, Lou. This is a once in a lifetime adventure for you, to say the least."

"Yeah, I think I kind of get it, but not really," said Louis. He felt confused and yet intrigued.

"I know it's a bit much to process, but if you end up working with us, you will learn more and more every day, and within a week you'll probably be able to explain the game better than myself. Who knows?" said Jack as he drank his coffee.

"Hmm, it's definitely interesting. I mean, I'm interested. Definitely. For sure," said Louis as they got to the lobby area of the building.

"Louis, if it's not for you, just say so. I wouldn't take it personally whatsoever. But if this is something you want to do, truly, then a one-month position could easily turn into a permanent thing, as long as you fit here, and we are both helping each other out. Your job, if you decide to take it, will be to test the game, and commit to helping us find out what works and what doesn't work, so we can fix any and all problems before it is launched publicly," Jack explained.

"If you don't mind my asking. What is the pay?"

After a pause that lasted a few seconds, but it seemed like minutes to Louis, Jack replied, "For one month's work?"

"Yes."

"Was waiting for you to ask, Louie," said Jack. "You would receive fifty thousand dollars for your first month with us, as well as benefits, and if you end up staying with us, loads of opportunity for advancement."

"Wait, did you just say, fifty grand?" asked Louis.

"That is correct," Jack responded.

"Well, damn. I'd have to be crazy to pass this up, wouldn't I? Shit. I barely made that all last year."

"That's funny. You're funny," said Jack.

There were a few moments of silence before Louis exclaimed, "So what's the catch? I mean there has to be a catch, right?" asked Louis.

"No catch, Louie. That is the pay."

"Is it like, dangerous or something?" asked Louis.

"As far as I know, no, it is not dangerous. Now, that is as of now, for the time being. But I can't promise you anything. Everything in life that is worth anything comes with a risk; you know what I'm saying? We gotta take big risks if we want big rewards, you know what I mean?" asked Jack.

"I think I do," said Louis as the job sounded better and better the more Jack explained it to him. Even if he could barely understand how it all worked, that was more money all at once than he had seen in a long time. And it would only take him a month. That money would help him solve at least some of the money problems he currently had, if not all of them.

"So, why don't I give you some time to think about it and then you can come back to me with your answer. But as of now, the job is yours if you want it."

Louis thought for a second before blurting out, "No. I mean yes, I mean...I'll take it. I don't think I'd be able to live with myself knowing that I turned this down. I'm your guy, Jack. Let's do this."

"Awesome. That's great to hear, Louie," said Jack as he started to smirk. "Now, the next step is that you have to sign a bunch of contracts, nondisclosure agreements, waivers, and so on."

"That's fine with me."

"Great," said Jack.

"Jack, if you don't mind me asking." Louis thought back to what his son said when he told him about his new potential position at Mindtrick. "Why me?"

"Well, to be honest, Louie, we already have the younger generation hooked on our games. The demographic we are trying to reach here is the older gamers. Those in your age group and even older. Those who used to play and fell out of love with videogames over time. Normal everyday guys, just like you, who just want to feel a sense of nostalgia and fun for once. This game gives you the ultimate feeling of nostalgia, almost overwhelming in some ways. Guys in your demographic are going to love this. I can almost guarantee it."

"I get it. I really do," said Louis as he looked around the lobby of the office building and still could not believe his eyes. It was all so surreal.

Jack reached out to shake his hand. "Come back next Monday and we'll have this all finalized, and you can start."

"I'll be here," said Louis as he shook Jack's hand. He was all smiles.

Chapter 5

Six days later, Louis sat on the couch in his apartment eating his favorite cereal, Frosty Puffs, and watching TV. Tomorrow would be the first day at his new job, so he planned to get to bed early.

He pulled out his phone and texted his son, Tommy. "Wish me luck. I start at Mindtrick tomorrow!"

After a couple of minutes, still no reply. Louis noticed that his phone was down to 9% of battery life. He walked over to the plug in the wall, then he looked at himself in the mirror.

He almost felt like a new man. Like maybe this could be his big break, or at least bigger than anything else he'd had going for him in a long time.

You got this, he thought as he plugged the charger into the bottom of his phone. He returned to his couch, picked up the remote control, and changed the channel to the local news at nine.

The big morning came. Louis was up at the crack of dawn. He got ready and made his way out the door in record time.

He truly felt that this was the first day of the rest of his life. Or at least the last day of whatever life he was currently living. Yesterday was in the past and he was ready for a new adventure. A well-paid adventure that he hoped would lead to a brand-new career in the videogame industry—the last field/industry that he'd ever seen himself getting into.

Louis pulled into the parking lot of the Mindtrick Games building. He stared at the big logo plastered on the outside walls of the large office space. The company made itself clearly visible and known to anyone that came downtown.

Luckily, Louis found an open guest parking spot since he had not yet been given his own parking space. He was trying to remind himself not to mess this one up. As he turned off his car, he felt his pocket vibrate. He took out his phone and saw a text from Tommy.

"Sorry I didn't see your message until now, GOOD LUCK DAD!" Another text immediately followed that said, "Give them hell!"

This made Louis smile. "Will do, boy," he wrote back.

He still was not exactly sure what his job duties would be. Louis was quite confused by most of what Jack had explained to him. But the money was too good to pass up. It also sounded fun the more that he contemplated it.

Louis walked in through the front doors with a sense of confidence he had not felt in a while. The receptionist said, "Hello, Mr. Parker. We've been awaiting your arrival."

"Oh, please, just call me Louie," he responded. "Do I have to sign in or anything?"

"Nope. Mr. Jack is waiting for you in his office. Good luck on your first day with us at Mindtrick. Louie." She smiled with a hypnotic set of eyes that Louis could not veer his away from. Then he snapped out of it.

"Thank you…"

"Emily," she said.

"Thank you, Emily. Glad to be here," said Louis. His palms started to sweat, and it all became more real as the moments went on.

Louis got lost on his way to Jack's office as he barely remembered anything from his last visit there. He walked by rooms that seemed so far ahead of their time with technology it did not even seem possible. One machine in a room by the break room had what looked like a dozen wires coming from it, and they were all connected to one person who must have been testing some sort of new product for the company.

After a couple of minutes, Louis was able to navigate himself close enough to hear Jack yell, "My guy! Big Louie in the house!" and drawing attention from anyone in sight. "This is our guy! This is the one! Everybody meet the chosen one. Louie Parker. We go way back. He's going to help us get *Seven Days* to the next level. Everyone better welcome that man and show him some damn respect, you hear?"

All of the coders and employees nodded as some of them walked up to introduce themselves. Anyone the boss called out like was important, and they all knew how much Mr. Jack had done not just for their careers, but in their opinion, for the world.

"Louie, when you get settled in, hit up my office. Judy! Get this damn man a coffee. He's one of us now!" Jack exclaimed as he walked back into his office and slammed the door shut.

"How do you like your coffee?" asked Judy.

"Well, actually, I don't drink the stuff."

Judy looked around nervously, then back at him. "Well, Mr. Jack thinks you should have a coffee so I'm going to get you one anyway. I'll try to make it the best cup of coffee I can! Nice to meet you!" she said as she ran over to the coffee maker in the break room.

"Oh...kay..." said Louis as he looked around at all the miraculous inventions and neat gaming tech. He was still in awe. He knew his son would love to see some of these projects the company was working on. Louis started to think that maybe he would finally be the cool Dad.

"Hi there. I'm Cody," said a young, shorter, thick man with square glasses and thick, black curly hair. "I'm one of the top coders here at Mindtrick. I'll be working closely with you on your progress in *Seven Days VR*. If you have any questions at all, big or small, I'm your guy."

"Nice to meet ya, Cody."

Judy ran back up to Louis and handed him a piping hot coffee in a red mug.

"Here you go, Mr. Parker," said Judy.

"Thank you. I appreciate that," said Louis as he smelled the coffee. When Judy left, he placed it on a table.

Another young man in a slick black suit walked up to Louis and stared him down before reaching out to shake his hand. "Hey, I'm Chris. I do viral and guerrilla marketing for the company. Hopefully by next year, I'll be head of the entire division. You are going to help us learn how to market to an older...I mean, *broader* audience. We're going to bring back gamers that haven't played in ages. You are our dinosaur, and we're going to metaphorically reverse your generation's extinction."

"Right...interesting...I think. Nice to meet you, Chris," said Louis as he became a little bit overwhelmed by all these new faces in such a different atmosphere than he was used to.

He retrieved his coffee cup and walked over towards Jack's office, looking around at the dozens of employees nearby. "I'm sure I'll meet all of you throughout the day. Gonna go see Jack now."

Louis made it to Jack's office. He knocked twice before opening the founder's door. Louis walked in. "You really hyped me up to them, huh?" he asked

"You are damn right I did,' said Jack. "How's the coffee? Just the way you like it I hope."

Louis looked down at his cup and responded, "It's perfect."

Jack got up out of his desk chair and looked out his window at the glorious view from his office. "Look, Louie, I know you're only doing this for the money. I get it. Trust me," he said as he walked over to his new hire and put his hand on his shoulder. "But I genuinely believe you are the man for the job. Just the guy we need. This game is going to be more important to people like…well, like you. Older. No disrespect. But I mean, young people play games at a staggering rate already. We want your generation's money, you know. Money to be able to make more games and change the world."

"No, that makes sense."

"Look, worst case scenario, it becomes too much for you to handle and you bail. We'll still pay you a prorated amount of what we promised you."

"Oh yeah? And best case?"

"This works like a charm, and you stay with us indefinitely and help us change the world. You can have an important role in the future of gaming as we know it, Lou," said Jack as he stepped away to take a sip of his coffee. "Man, that's good shit."

"You guys really like changing the world, huh?" said Louis.

"Who the hell doesn't?" Jack responded.

"Right."

Jack walked back to his computer desk and took a seat. "So, listen. You won't be doing what you were hired to do officially until at least next week. This week, we'll get through the paperwork. Then I'll have Cody show you the ropes, the ins and outs. Get you prepared for the official trial run."

"I'm all yours."

"That's my guy! That's what I like to hear! A true company man right here," said Jack. "You're going to fit in just fine, my friend. Welcome to the Mindtrick family."

Chapter 6

Louis received a text message from his ex-wife, Denise. It read, "I still haven't gotten your child support payment this month."

He rolled his eyes and texted back, "I just landed a new gig. I should be able to send your check in a couple of days, Denise."

"K and can you take the kids Friday? Me and Shawn are going out," Denise wrote.

"I think I have to work Friday, but I'll let you know."

"K… if not, no biggie," she replied.

Louis threw his phone across his apartment and went downstairs to his mailbox in hopes his first check had arrived early from Mindtrick Games. It had not. He was told he would receive his first check in the mail, and most of his future checks would be direct deposited.

"Dammit!" he muttered as he slammed his mailbox shut.

Louis went back up the three floors to his apartment. He picked up the remote control for the television and turned it on. He watched a commercial for another Mindtrick game called Stellar Radio Funk. A game his son had been talking about for months. The graphics were superb, and the gameplay looked quite addicting.

The next day, Louis was at the Mindtrick Games office building, awaiting word from Cody on when they would get started. Cody had said he had a bit of last-minute quantum coding to do ahead of Louis' training.

Louis waited patiently and watched the clock tick slower and slower for almost an hour until Cody finally said, "Let's get started."

Cody handed over a two-inch thick book that was titled, "Project Seven." Louis looked at it for a second and realized he had not read an actual book in years, and this manual was bigger than anything he may have ever read in his lifetime.

"Over the next week or so, you are going to learn a lot, and it will be nearly impossible to remember it all. So, when something is crucial to the process and important to remember, I will say a code word. Write this down: the code word is '*high tide*'. If I ever say those words, you must pay close attention. I know this is all like a brand-new world to you, so I'll try to explain everything as simply as possible," Cody went on.

"I will do my absolute best," Louis responded.

"That's all we can do, right?" said Cody as he pulled a chalkboard closer and placed it upright. Then he grabbed a piece of chalk and started to write on the board.

"Right," said Louis as he listened closely to what the young coder was saying. He was eager and nervous, yet excited. He had no idea what to expect.

After a long first day of training, Cody had filled the chalkboard with equations and codes that Louis had dutifully copied into his notebook. Louis tried his best to comprehend the technology and almost convinced himself that he understood it all more than he actually did.

"So, I get to go back to any day I've ever lived in my life and relive it. Really? Up to seven days?"

"Correct. Those are the test parameters. And you can't do the same day twice. The trial days must be spread out with a couple days in between, maybe more, so we can analyze the results and data, and try to catch anything we need to fix. Like glitches and quirks in the gameplay we couldn't see in the production stage. With your trial, we will be able to finish developing the final last-minute details. You must keep your eyes open and you must try to not fall asleep while you are inside the virtual environment," Cody explained.

"Whoa, sounds…intense," said Louis. He was trying to make sure he was hearing Cody correctly. It all sounded very sci-fi and futuristic. He did not even think this type of thing was possible. Maybe a hundred years from now, but definitely not today. The technology just seemed so alien to Louis. It all struck him as pretty magical at first glance.

"The entire video game tests the laws of quantum mechanics which nobody really understands in the first place. Not only is the game fully immersive, but it is also self-correcting as well," Cody went on.

"How is this even possible?" asked Louis.

"Once we upload your memories and subconscious to the cloud, the sky is the limit. It's hard to explain, but just remember that once you get started...try to have fun. Okay, let's pick back up tomorrow. I'm pooped," said Cody.

"Sounds good," Louis responded.

Louis was not scheduled to have his kids until Friday, but he was eager to tell Tommy about his new gig. He doubted he would even believe it. He barely believed it himself.

On his ride home from work, Louis turned up the radio to listen to one of his favorite rock songs. He began to jam out in the car. He lit a cigarette and sang the lyrics at the top of his lungs. He inhaled the smoke as it filled the back of his car before exiting through the cracked windows.

He was happy to finally be able to smoke in his car without having to worry about passengers getting mad about it. Since he had this new position, he was optimistic that he would not have to go back to working for Ryder. At least not anytime soon.

Louis got a text from a beautiful woman named Karen whom he had been texting lately. He met her on a new dating app called SoulMate. The ironic part of the name is that very few people actually found their soul mates on there. More like horrible first dates and drunken one-night stands. He had not gotten anymore texts or calls from Tina, so he figured he might as well see who else was out there that he could date.

Karen wanted him to take her barhopping, but Louis was exhausted from training at work. He also had to be up bright and early to do it again the next day.

He told her he needed a raincheck for another time. She was not too thrilled with his decision and sent him a couple of angry face emojis to make that clear. He did not care since all he was worried about was his new job and trying to keep it.

After the first few days of training, Louis was slowly but surely starting to grasp the concept of *Seven Days VR*.

Cody walked into the lab and joined Louis. He brought him a piping hot cup of coffee.

"Today, we will be training in actual virtual reality," Cody said as he took a sip from his own cup.

"Okay," Louis responded as he also took a drink. "Hot."

"It's always hot. Jack doesn't accept anything less. It's pretty weird actually."

"That man just loves his coffee, I guess," said Louis.

"So today, just...be cool. You're going to witness things that you never thought were possible. This console is the best of the best, top of the line VR you can find. This specific model isn't even available yet. It will be released a week before *Seven Days* goes on the market so users can experience the game the best way possible," Cody explained.

Louis prepared himself by doing a series of stretches. Then he sat down so Cody could put the VR headset on his head and strap it, making sure it fit him properly. When it covered his eyes, Louis could not see a thing. He started to freak out. It brought him back to his own childhood for a second, when he was really young. Louis was quite afraid of the dark.

"Relax," said Cody as he handed Louis two gloves. "Put these on so you can control your avatar. After some minutes, the server will coordinate the settings to sync the headset and controller gloves together. When you play the actual game, you'll have to upload your consciousness. You'll learn more about that next week. But for now, let's get you used to the virtual world."

Cody flipped a switch on the headset and pressed a button on the console. The gloves lit up and moments later the darkness slowly filled with light, getting brighter and brighter. Louis closed his eyes to adjust to the changes in his vision.

Seconds went by and Louis opened his eyes and looked around inside the headset. He found himself in a mesmerizing tropical beach setting. The graphics were quite vivid. As his eyes adjusted, Louis began to see himself through first person. He waved his hands in front of his face, and they looked so real. He had never imagined graphics so clean and crisp. He looked around in a 360-degree spin to see the colorful beach scenery. He knew he was experiencing something truly special. He thought to himself, *This is going to change the world. Jack was right.*

"This is amazing," Louis said as he started to walk around slowly.

The graphics were so stunning that, as time moved forward, Louis almost began to believe it was real.

"It's incredible," he said as he moved his arms around so he could see himself some more. His mind was racing almost as fast as his heart. His avatar was wearing a black and orange jumpsuit with a Mindtrick logo stamped on the chest. Louis walked over to the ocean water. He gazed down at his reflection. Instead of a VR headset, the reflection showed smooth metallic goggles covering his eyes. His hair was spiked up and his beard had more volume to it.

Louis started to run in the water…until he crashed into the wall of the lab.

"Oh right, sorry," said Cody. "*High tide*. You can't run freely until next week when we get you in the virtual room for the first day of the trial run. This training room isn't equipped with all of the right sensors to keep you in the game's vortex. But don't worry, you're doing great."

"Right," said Louis getting up off the ground trying to find his balance. He was still adjusting to the visual and physical aspect of it all.

"I don't even care. This is so damned cool," said Louis.

The weekend came and with it the visit from Louis' kids. He had his mind in the clouds thinking about his new job and anticipating what was to come. But the presence of his kids brought him back to the moment at hand.

"Tommy, go get your sister from outside and tell her dinner is ready," said Louis.

"One second. I'm about to reach my highest score in Snow Worms," said Tommy. "Shit!" he yelled, "Just lost!"

"Okay. Now go get your sister," said Louis as he checked the tuna casserole and took the plates out of the cabinet. He cleaned off the kitchen table to get ready for dinner.

Tommy ran down the stairs and out the apartment to find his sister on the phone with her best friend. "Hey, Dad says get upstairs, we're about to have dinner."

"Coming," she said. "I gotta call you back, Becca…gotta eat with my Dad and annoying ass brother."

"Tell Becca I said what's up," said Tommy.

"No, loser," she said. "Bye Becca," Natalie said. She hung up her video call and followed her brother inside.

"You're so annoying," she said. "I hope you know that."

"Oh, I do," said Tommy as he pushed her into the wall. "Watch out!" he said, laughing.

"Asshole!" she yelled before slapping the back of his head as they ran up the apartment building stairs.

Louis and his kids ate their dinner together in peace. They had the same tuna casserole that Louis had been making for years. The kids would not get off their phones. But at least he was spending time with them.

He cleared his throat and said, "Hey…what's the difference between a guitar and tuna fish?"

"What?" said Tommy as he played on his phone.

"You can tune a guitar, but you can't tune a fish," said Louis.

Tommy actually laughed for a moment before his sister said, "That was absolutely horrible, Father."

Chapter 7

Today was the big day. His first day of the trial run of *Seven Days VR*.

Louis woke up to his alarm going off on his phone. He jumped out of bed and hopped in the shower. Louis felt like he was as ready as he would ever be for this new job.

It all still felt a little too good to be true, but he figured he had nothing to lose. He really enjoyed seeing some real money in his checking account for the first time in years as the company already sent him a check for five thousand dollars. He also concluded that if something went wrong and they harmed him in any way, he could sue them for all they were worth. Louis signed all the forms; he did not exactly read his contracts and liability forms word for word. But again, he had nothing to lose. He was not scared, just excited. This was exactly the type of thing he needed to spice up his life. He also felt like he could trust his younger brother's old friend, Jack.

He finished up in the shower before he shaved his beard shorter to look more professional. Then he brushed his teeth until they were sparkling white and gargled with some mouthwash.

Louis decided to wear his best suit, hoping to make a good impression on the big day. He knew he would have to change before the game started but he wanted to impress everyone when he arrived. He was ready to show the company that he was serious about his new role and grateful to be there.

Before Louis walked through the front door of Mindtrick Games, he decided to have a cigarette. He lit it up with his purple lighter and tried to blow the smoke away from his suit, so he would not reek of cigarette smoke.

Louis greeted Emily in the lobby before he made his way down the long halls. He finally arrived at the main lab.

He walked inside and saw Jack, Cody, and the project's team of coders standing around.

"Louie!" Jack exclaimed as he walked over and shook his hand before hugging him. "Today, we make history. Well, you know… change it too, hah-hah!"

"That is it!" said Louis. "Hey, Cody."

"Hey Louie."

"Cody and the team are going to bring you to the virtual room and get you all set up. Can't wait to see how it goes. This is my baby, Louie," Jack said with a grin.

"I'm here for this, Jack. I won't let you down," Louis replied. Jack put his hand on Louis' shoulder.

"That's my man," said the boss. "All right, what are we waiting for?"

"Let's do this," said Cody.

"Lead the man to his new office, or shall I say, virtual office," said Jack. "I'm counting on all of you. You are a team. Good luck, Louie. We're going to change the world with this one, bud."

"Sure are," said Louie as he followed Cody and the group out the door and down the hallway towards the large virtual room.

The virtual room was accessible only to authorized personnel. Cody swiped his keycard and let the computer scan his eye before the large door finally opened. "This way," Cody said to Louis as he pointed inside the brightly lit room.

The virtual room took up nearly half of the building. "This is the real lab," said Cody.

Louis looked down at the blue and green panels on the floor beside each wall. "What are those?" he asked, pointing.

"So, when you get near the out-of-bounds range, or better yet, the virtual walls, the ground sensor will turn you in the direction you need to go to keep running. If you are running, that is. The floors and the walls will also sync up to different large objects or buildings, letting you jump off or run up. You won't notice the difference while in the game," Cody went on.

"That's...incredible," Louis responded.

"Yes, yes, it is," said Cody.

Louis went to the locker room to change into something more comfortable. He threw on a plain white tee-shirt and some basketball shorts. Cody told him he could wear whatever he wanted. Before he went back, Louis stopped and looked in the mirror. *What are you getting yourself into, Lou?* he asked himself.

He returned to the large lab to join Cody and the team.

Then they prepared the virtual room for the trial run of *Seven Days VR*. The team got Louis in his equipment, adjusting his headset and controller gloves to a perfect fit.

When he was all ready to go, his heart raced like a horse on a track. It was now or never. He knew this was his chance to prove himself. He took a deep breath.

"Now is the time we upload your consciousness. It's nearly painless. It will only last for about thirty seconds and once it's done, we can start the game. This is a major key in jumpstarting the quantum regulator, which is what allows you to go back in time to your very own memories," said Cody.

"Do what you gotta do, my friend," said Louis.

One of the team members brought out a machine with wires connected to it. One wire was blue and the other four were black. They had suctions at the end of them.

Louis watched as the freaky technology was handed off to Cody.

"Okay, let's get this over with," Cody said as he took the first wire and placed it on top of Louis' head. He then hooked up the other four, one on his forehead, one on his neck, and two on different parts of his brain that were pertinent to the algorithm and gameplay.

They pulled a lever on the machine that was connected by wires and then pushed down a couple of red buttons. These wires were also attached to Louis's head. A jolt of energy went back and forth from Louis to the machine. This mechanism allowed for the program to upload all of the player's memories, consciousness, thought patterns, and scan the brain entirely.

Louis started screaming, "Ahh!"

"Relax," said Cody. "Almost done."

"Dammit!" yelled Louis.

Thirty-five seconds later, it was over. Louis opened his eyes to realize he was already in virtual reality. All the team was out of sight. Someone pulled off the wires.

"Louie, can you hear me?" asked Cody into the loudspeaker of the virtual room.

"Yeah, I can," Louis responded as he acclimated to the virtual environment.

"Louie, I need to know what date you want to relive for the first level," said Cody.

"Right," said Louis.

"Listen, if you can't remember specific dates, the game can figure it out based on keywords transmitted by your uploaded memory."

"Okay. I think, lemme think," Louis stalled as he looked around at the magical four-dimensional reality he had transported into.

"Maybe make it something simple, take it easy for Day One. We still got many more to go in the trial," Cody said.

"Take me back to when I was fifteen, Thanksgiving!" Louis exclaimed.

"You got it, chief," said Cody as he typed in "Thanksgiving" and "age fifteen".

The date came up as November 23, 1995. Cody pressed "Enter" on his laptop keyboard that was connected to the entire game database.

Louis fell toward the time portal. He felt like he was being sucked through a tunnel as he traveled through space and time with stars flying past him at the speed of light. He felt weightless for a moment until he landed on his feet, regaining his balance. He found himself in front of his childhood home.

He looked around. The parked cars all looked like older models. Then he realized he was in the nineties. 1995 to be exact.

This is insane, he said to himself.

Louis walked in the front door of his parents' house and they all greeted him with love.

His mother yelled out, "Finally! We thought you biked to Jordie's house. Food is almost ready, pumpkin."

"Yes, Mom, sorry," said Louis. His big sister, Kelly, walked by wearing jean overalls. He could not believe what he was seeing. It really worked. Louis had gone back in time, even if it was all simulated through a videogame. It felt so real to him. The sounds, the smells, it all came back to him.

"Hey, scrub," Kelly said as she nudged Louis.

"Happy…Thanksgiving?" Louis said, completely astonished. He couldn't take his eyes from his beloved sister. In his real life, Kelly had been gone for more than twenty years, killed in a car crash.

Louis had selected this memory because it was the last time that he could remember his entire family getting along. Before everyone seemed to drift apart and lose touch after years of fighting with one another. It all got much worse when Kelly died. His father, Clyde, and his mother, Dawn, were fighting nearly every night until they finally got a divorce. Louis wanted a chance to relive this happier moment before his family fell apart.

He sat down at the dinner table with his parents, as well as his sister, Kelly, and his two brothers, Roy and Connor. They ate and laughed as Clyde told stories about the kids when they were toddlers. The family even got a game of football going in the backyard. Louis could not believe how real the game felt. The graphics, the environment, the simulation did not feel simulated. He felt like he had free will. He soon forgot he was playing a videogame at all. He could not believe a game could feel so authentic and eerily familiar.

Chapter 8

The next day, while he was standing outside on his lunch break, a flock of birds flew above Louis. He watched their graceful soaring. He imagined that flying like them must be amazing. Then he thought about how it might have gotten tiring after a while, always being in the air like that. He wondered if he would be able to fly in *Seven Days VR*. Nothing seemed beyond the realm of possibility after experiencing one day in the game. Louis was deathly afraid of flying in airplanes, but the birds were close enough that they did not seem that high off the ground. The birds circled in the air before heading west into the distance. Louis waved to them as they disappeared behind a few tall buildings downtown, then had a cigarette before heading back inside.

He walked into the lab and saw Cody flipping through pages with a smile on his face. "These results are amazing," said Cody.

Louis looked at the computer monitors on the wall but could not understand a lick of what any of it meant.

Cody went on, "Oh, and *high tide*. The algorithm really works on another level in many ways. It appears the system is processing faster than we ever could have expected. Which is a good thing, considering the amount of memory the campaign mode took up. So, we have room to work with updating the graphics just a tad bit more.

"What is most fascinating to me, however, is the fact that the game recreates your memories so clearly. It's almost as if it was there when it happened or something. I'll show you what I mean in a little bit and you can tell me if you agree or not, but so far…the technology is proving to work. And after weeks of monitoring you, we'll be able to know for certain that it's safe for consumers to use. But as of now, I am stunned by what I'm seeing. Truly. Jack was right. You were a great candidate for this position, I must say. Even if he and I don't always agree on everything, he was right about this one. I'll give him that."

"That's great to hear," said Louis.

"One thing that caught my eye was that you relived your day almost entirely the same as you did the first time around. It proved many things. Like for instance, you would rather just relive the moment how it was rather than try to change it in the slightest. At least when it's a moment that you hold close to your heart and cherish deeply, it seems." Cody read through more pages of results.

"Well, I don't know. It was the first day. I figured I wouldn't jump in the deep end just yet without testing the waters. You know?" said Louis.

"That's fine. I get it. But listen. Maybe try to get a bit more action in the next day of trials. Not saying go crazy, just stir it up a bit, so we can study results that push the game to its limits and truly test out the system and algorithm. You catch my drift?" said Cody as turned to the next page.

"I think I get it," said Louis.

"But so far, so good," said Cody.

"That's good to hear. This shit is impressive, I must say. At times, it felt like it was real...like, I don't even know how to explain it, really," said Louis.

"That's normal for your first day," said Cody.

"Gotcha. Next one will be more interesting. I'll think of something good," said Louis.

"We'll return to the lab in two days. Get some rest and get some food in you," said Cody as he sat down at his computer and began to type.

"Sounds good," said Louis.

On his way out the door, Emily stopped Louis and handed him an envelope.

"Mr. Jack wanted me to give you this," she said.

"Thank you, Emily," he said as he put it in his pocket. "Have a great day."

"Have a great day, handsome," she replied and smiled before looking him up and down. She then returned to her desk and picked up the phone to make a call. She waved at Louis one more time. He waved back.

Damn, he thought to himself as he walked out the front door of Mindtrick Games.

When he got outside, he tore open the envelope to find a check for ten thousand dollars.

"Yes!" yelled Louis. He also found a note from Jack that read, "Little Starting Bonus for my main man, Louie.—Mr. Jack."

"Thank you, Mr. Jack," Louis said to himself as he looked closely at Jack's signature. "That's what I'm talking about!"

Two days later, Louis was back at the Mindtrick Games building in downtown San Diego. He paced back and forth as he prepared to get transported again into the world of *Seven Days VR*. He planned on having a very productive second day of trials.

"Where are we going today, boss dog?" asked Cody as he handed Louis a steaming cup of hot coffee.

"Thanks," Louis said as he took it and sipped it almost immediately.

He did not get as much sleep as he hoped for as he was too excited about the second day in the game.

"Any ideas? If it were me in your position, I'd be making diagrams and graphs trying to decide what days to relive. It is a lot of pressure, I know that. Tough making up your mind. Who can even pick seven days out of their entire life they want to experience again?" Cody went on.

"Night of my senior prom," Louis responded promptly.

"Oh. Nice!" said Craig, one of the team members. Craig was incredibly smart with a sense of naiveté for a thirty-year-old man. "You going back because it sucked? Or you are going back to prom because it was the bomb?"

"That was the night I lost my virginity, and it was awful," said Louis.

"That makes sense," said Cody.

"It is what it is, I suppose. Maybe if we get to that point you guys could like look the other way or something?" said Louis.

"Yeah, don't worry. I'll make sure the guys don't look," Cody said before laughing.

Jack walked into the virtual lab. "My dream team!"

"Mr. Jack. Welcome," said Craig.

"Shut up, Craig. How are you, Lou?" asked Jack.

"I'm good, man," Louis responded even though he was feeling quite nervous to say the least.

"I went over the results from Day One. Very impressive, Louie," said Jack.

"I appreciate that," Louis said.

"Let's make Day Two even better. What do you say?" the founder asked with a big grin on his face.

"Let's do it," said Louis.

Jack put his hand up for a high five until Louis slapped it.

"Woo!" yelled Jack as he left the room. "Big things, boys! We're doing big things!"

"Anyway," said Cody. "Got you all set up. Whenever you're ready, dude."

"I'm ready," said Louis.

The team assisted Louis in getting his equipment on. Once he was all set up, Cody pushed "Start" and then "Enter" for the day and year. And the game began.

Louis spawned just outside the high school with his date, Becky Bishop, on his arm. They were walking inside with their friends Tanya, Maggie, Lester, and Richie.

He'd met Becky when they both were smoking cigarettes while skipping chemistry class a month prior to the prom. One day, he finally asked her to go with him, and she said, "sure," mostly, he suspected, because she did not have a date yet.

They walked through the halls that led to the school gymnasium. Popular songs from 1997 got louder and louder as Louis and his friends approached the basketball court.

After hours of dancing, Louis tried the various life skills he'd learned since high school to impress Becky more than he did the first time around. This time he had smoother dance moves and sung along with some of his favorite songs of all time, most of which were now considered oldies or classics. But back then, they were the hottest songs out. The crowd of high schoolers began to go wild when the song "Booty Jungle" came on through the speakers.

When prom ended, the group went back to Lester's parents' house where they would continue partying in the basement. Lester knew where his parents hid the liquor.

Louis made all the right moves on the way home in the back of Richie's convertible. His date, Becky, kissed him the entire time.

In the basement, the boys were trying to get lucky with their prom dates. Louis thought he was doing the best out of all of them, considering he had a lifetime of experience and knowledge this time around. However, he was still as nervous as ever. He had been teleported back in time to one of the most regretful nights of his life. He had always wanted a do-over. However, maybe things were better off left the way they were.

Louis started to drink at a faster pace. He thought because he was older in real life that he had a higher tolerance. But since he was a lightweight in the VR game, that was what his virtual player could handle.

He got wasted and ended up blacking out for a half an hour before waking up and puking in the nearest waste basket.

While he was passed out, Becky called one of her older brothers to come pick her up.

"I have to go," said Becky as she grabbed her tiny pink designer purse and headed up the stairs and out of the basement. With puke on his tuxedo, Louis followed her outside where her two brothers were waiting for her, leaning against their car.

One of them, the bigger of the two, said, "Is this the asshole?"

"Don't do it, Zander!" Becky yelled.

Louis, not sure what was going on, still trying to get a hold of himself, looked over at the brothers as they got closer. His vision blurred as they approached him.

Just then, the heavier brother, Zander, rocked Louis with a punch to the nose so hard he could feel the bones shifting in his face. Louis dropped to the ground as the other brother, also humungous in size, started stomping on Louis. The pain was real. Or at least it felt real. He knew it, even though he was plastered drunk. This was surely sobering him up in the game. His friend Lester finally broke it up.

After the brothers stomped him, they jumped back into their car and took off with Becky. Louis was left on the ground, bleeding from his nose.

Louis was on the ground for nearly ten minutes in excruciating pain. He looked up at the sky and noticed that the clouds started to glitch. They began to move horizontally, and then vertically, while vibrating back and forth.

"What the hell?" Louis asked himself as he gazed at the weird night sky dancing before his eyes.

Back at the Mindtrick office building, the coders were busy trying to figure out what was causing the glitch in the game.

"I have a feeling that the disc is scratched," said Cody as he sat down at his laptop and started typing code into the keyboard to collaborate the algorithm. But nothing seemed to work. The graphics blurred, and the colors transformed on the screen. They were concerned for Louis' health if he stayed in the game for much longer.

"Pull the plug!" yelled Cody. He decided to cut their losses and get Louis out of the game before too much damage was done to his brain.

Back in the VR game, Louis hoped that he would be all right as the sky began to fall around him. He looked over at some trees waving back and forth as the leaves on the branches turned turquoise. The road lit up bright orange. He sat up and rubbed his eyes in disbelief.

Just then, the level ended, and Louis was greeted back in the virtual room. The team checked on him to make sure he was all right, running tests and monitoring his vital signs. Dr. Herman ran in to run more specialized tests on Louis. He was the company doctor, only ever called upon when there were medical emergencies in the office.

"What the hell happened?" asked Louis as he regained his awareness of reality.

Cody walked over to the console and pressed the eject button. He studied the Seven Days game disc.

"Aha! I knew it," said Cody.

"What?" asked Louis as a coder handed him a bottle of water.

"Disc was scratched. That's why everything started to look weird and glitched out on you. I called it," Cody said.

Chapter 9

"Well, that was a bad idea," said Louis, as he watched Cody go over the previous day's results.

"Man, you're a trooper, Louie," said Cody. "I got to run some of this by Jack. I'll be back shortly. Get some rest. You just had a traumatizing experience, my dude."

"I'm fine," said Louis as he sat there, pondering the last level he played wondering where he went wrong.

"Be back soon. And don't worry. It is just a game. In real life, you still lost your virginity after prom and you still only lasted two minutes. It happens to the best of us, big man," said Cody as he left the lab.

"Very funny." Louis stood up just before getting a big headache. He sat back down as blood rushed to his brain.

Louis was still trying to accept the fact that he was the chosen one for this project. He had his few doubts. But the money was coming in, and the cash was real even if the way he made it seemed like the exact opposite. He was beginning to wonder if he was actually already living in some sort of simulation. He had heard that theory before. Now it was starting to make more sense.

He sat around at the office as he waited for further instructions from Cody. He watched the young coders around him working intently on their laptops. They appeared to be in a trance, typing away. He could only imagine what they were doing, what they were working on—if it had to do with him, or if it was another new groundbreaking game that would, as Jack put it, change the world.

No matter how much he tried to take it all in, it all felt inexplicable. He could not even describe the experience to his son. Tommy thought he was exaggerating. Louis tried explaining that it felt like he was living in some sort of movie or TV show.

Louis never thought he would reach the point in his life where he'd find his purpose. But now he was starting to think this might be it. That he was, in fact, chosen. He just was not exactly sure why. However, he was not complaining. Louis was getting paid to play videogames, something he never even thought was possible.

On his next day off, Louis decided to go to the mall with his new credit card and a nice chunk of cash in his hand.

He had all of his bills paid including his child support. Because of that, and with more money coming in any day now, he thought he could treat himself for once.

He went around to all sorts of stores, many of which he had never stepped foot in before.

He bought himself a brand-new suit as well as new shoes, a tie, and designer sunglasses. Then he found the videogame store and bought his son five brand new videogames. From there, he went into the jewelry store and picked out a beautiful bracelet for his daughter with real diamonds on it. He could finally afford to pay nearly five hundred dollars for a single bracelet…so he figured he'd live it up and spoil his children a bit.

Later that week, it was Day Three of the trial run for *Seven Days VR*. Louis felt like he was finally getting the hang of it.

"Today, I want to go back to my high school football championship. The day I missed the game-winning touchdown catch. Worst day of my life. I know I can make that touchdown if I just get one more shot. So why the hell not?" said Louis.

"Sounds like a plan," said Cody as he prepared the virtual room for the game.

After everything was all set up, Cody searched for the memory using the keywords "football", "high school", and "championship" and it came up instantly.

The game updated itself every time they ran the beta. It almost knew Louis from head to toe at this point.

"You ready, Louie?" Cody asked.

"Ready," Louis responded.

Cody pushed "Start" on the game and hit "Enter" on the keyboard for the date January 10, 1997.

Months before the senior prom, the championships were the biggest deal in the history of sports at Jefferson High School.

Louis was still a somewhat popular kid for a misfit. He made a name for himself on the football team as one of the best, if not the best, wide receivers on the team. He made it to varsity by his sophomore year of high school. He used football as his escape from all of the drama back at home.

The game had begun, and Louis was playing even better than he had the first time around. He was in the body of his teenage self but had the mindset of a veteran on the field. He was making plays he never could have made back then. The crowd was loving it. His parents were in the stands cheering him on with his brothers and sister.

After a close back and forth game with their division rivals, it came down to the last minute of the fourth quarter. It was almost time for the big play that he had botched the first time.

The quarterback, Tyson Buckman, called the exact same play, a reverse slant toward the goal post. He signaled to Louis that he would be looking for him. Louis got incredibly nervous as the huddle came to a break and it was time.

The ball was hiked, and Louis took off. He knew that he'd missed the catch the first time because he looked back for the catch too soon, and the cornerback on the other team got an interception that resulted in a touchdown. This time, Louis went the same route but took his time to avoid messing up again.

Louis got close to the cornerback just before pivoting to the left—and then looking back.

At the last second, Louis grabbed the ball out of the air from behind and dove into the end zone. He got the touchdown. With only seconds left in the game, they were able to stop the other team from scoring again. The team celebrated and threw Louis up in the air for making the game-winning catch. He now knew more than ever before that he had missed out on something great. The memory was so vivid and precious this time around. He just wished it was real. He wished that when he left the game, that the real world would remember him as a winner, as a champion.

Since he still had sixteen hours to go in this Day Three trial level, he figured he would embrace the love he was getting from his peers, classmates, teammates, and pretty much the entire city.

He went to the after-party, and then the next morning got welcomed and "high fived" at school by everyone he walked past.

"Totally worth it," Louis said to himself as he readied for this third day in the videogame to come to an end.

Chapter 10

All Louis wanted was a micro-dose of sleep. He seemed to be getting less and less as the days went on. And his body was feeling the effects.

It was the weekend, and he was tossing and turning, waking up nearly every hour on the hour. Nothing would help, even after he drank nearly twenty ounces of cough syrup.

His mind was racing. He was restless, as well as overly anxious. It could be a side effect of the game. He was spending a lot of time in *Seven Days*. And with no previous tests done, nobody really knew the risks that the new and innovative game could potentially have. But he was enjoying it for the most part. He just could not get back to sleep. His body and mind would not let him no matter how much he tried.

His dreams were more vivid than usual and once he woke up, they all felt real. But most of his dreams were just various memories from his past, so technically they were real. Or at least as real as he could remember them.

After waking up for the third time that night, Louis finally decided to make himself a late-night snack to preoccupy his mind and belly for a little bit.

He made a double-decker peanut butter and jelly sandwich, just like he'd done for Tommy and Natalie when they were young. He also grabbed a bowl of chocolate ice cream and sat on his couch to watch some television before trying to go back to bed.

He scrolled through channels only finding random infomercials until he finally found a station with some cartoons. He started to think about his dreams and wondered, again, if his new gig was the cause of it. He never had dreams like those before.

I don't care. At least I'm finally making some real money, he decided. *Just gotta keep telling myself that.*

Days later, back at Mindtrick Games, Louis waited in the virtual room for Cody and the rest of the team to arrive. He was ready to start Day Four of the beta version of *Seven Days VR.*

"Sorry we're late. We were finishing another project, similar to this one," said Cody as he and the remaining team members walked in the large, illuminated room.

"No problem," said Louis as he tried to keep his eyes open. He was exhausted, but he did not want to make too much of an issue about it. He thought he could get through the level. He figured he would take a long nap when he was done with his shift.

"I'll be right back. Need to step out for a second," said Louis as he walked outside to have a cigarette. He then realized he had no idea what date to go back to for the fourth day. He tried to think long and hard, but nothing stood out to him.

When he got back inside, he went up to Cody.

"So, I don't know what day to pick. How about you just pick one for me? Dealer's choice," said Louis while he started to laugh nervously.

"Actually, that's not a bad idea. I've studied some important memories from your upload. I think we can pick a good day for you to relive. Might even be more fun not knowing before going into it. I like it. Let's do it," said Cody as he put a clipboard down on the ground and started setting up the VR console.

Cody plugged in the date: March 25, 2007.

Once Louis was set, he gave Cody the thumbs up signal. Then Cody pressed "Enter" on the date and started the next level.

After transporting through the virtual vortex, Louis spawned in Times Square.

At first, he could not place the day this memory represented. He looked to the right and saw his brother, Roy. Then it all started to come back to him. This was the night Louis wanted to take Roy to a night club in New York City for Roy's 21sr birthday. But they'd gotten into a petty argument after dinner, and Louis ended up leaving his brother and getting a taxi back to his friend's apartment uptown.

They walked up and down the streets of Manhattan. And then, Roy said the very same thing that started their fight the first time.

"You know, if you play your cards right tonight, you may actually have a real conversation with a lady. A real live lady," said Roy as he laughed and pushed Louis towards the street.

Louis remembered that it was his response that escalated it. He knew deep down his brother was just messing around. So instead of overreacting, this time Louis said. "You may be right."

Roy paused in his tracks and stood still for a moment. He looked at Louis and said, "Nice. I don't know why I thought that would piss you off, but I thought it would. Let's have a killer night!"

They went to a restaurant and proceeded to have the night of their lives. Louis was surprised at how great it really was. He could not believe he missed out on the experience the first time.

He was having a blast with his brother on Roy's 21st birthday. They were taking shots and talking to beautiful women at the pub before they made their way to a nearby night club. Louis wanted his brother's first night of legal drinking to be remembered as something special.

Roy told everyone at the club that it was his birthday. Girls started to dance on him and Louis because of it. At one point, three girls danced with Louis at the same time. He looked over at his brother who gave him a wink. Louis let out a burst of laughter as he took a shot of whiskey and slammed it on the table of the night club.

As the night went on, they stopped at a couple of other clubs and bars down the street. They finally wound up at a strip club after the bars started closing for the night.

Louis stepped outside to have a smoke. He could not believe he had missed out on this experience. He wondered what else he'd missed, and if he and his brother could have mended their relationship a long time ago.

This is nuts, Louis thought to himself.

The two stayed at the club until it closed at four in the morning. Somehow, Roy was able to get one of the strippers to let them crash with her and her friend, who was also a dancer there.

They walked back to her apartment, stumbling over themselves. Roy started to run down the street before tripping over the curb and falling hard on his face.

Louis lit up a cigarette and took a couple of puffs just before his girl, who called herself Passion, took it out of his mouth and took a few drags herself.

Roy's girl, Summer, had tattoos from head to toe and when she walked, her booty would shake back and forth like a pendulum.

The brothers felt larger than life, going home with two dancers. This was something Louis had never done before.

He was having fun. This could turn out to be one of the best moments he could remember, even if it was just part of a video game in the end. He was lost in it. It felt more real than anything during the moment. With this vixen of a woman, Sparkle, on his arm…Louis began to wonder why he did not have more wild and crazy nights like this. He got over it, and just tried to enjoy the moment for what it was. A memory that he and his brother could have had forever. But for now, it was only a simulation. One that Louis may have been enjoying way too much.

Chapter 11

A few days later, Louis felt like he was still trying to recover from his fourth day of game trials. The hangover from the game crept over into reality and Louis could feel it for quite some time afterwards. When the level was over, he had gone home and finally slept...for twenty hours straight. He woke up to nine missed calls, a dozen texts, and voicemails from his job, ex-wife, and children wondering where he was.

In front of his apartment building, Louis lit a cigarette with his red lighter. He watched from the sidewalk as cars went by. He felt rejuvenated, to say the least, from catching up on sleep after the previous week's intense activities. The game had been taking a toll on him in ways he was beginning to notice, and others were too, changes that he was still unaware of entirely.

He inhaled the smoke before letting it back out. He checked his phone to make sure he was not late to work. He had a couple of hours until he was supposed to clock in.

Louis thought he may have been sensing a few health-related side effects from all the time he had been spending in virtual reality. Besides insomnia, he'd noticed a dull headache.

He took a drag of his cigarette before flicking it into the road. He got into his car and took off towards the office. He drove by a billboard with an advertisement for a new game called Killnoise. It was made by none other than Mindtrick Games.

Louis entered the Mindtrick building and headed to the lab to start work. He was prepared to spend the next twenty-four hours in the game.

It was Day Five of the trial run and Louis was all set and ready to play. He was starting to get the hang of it and was showing more and more spirit as the experiment progressed. He felt like he was doing something important. And no matter what happened next, he decided he would not regret a thing. He thought he was on the way to beating the game with impressive results for Mindtrick to analyze for years to come. He felt like he was the chosen one. He felt like a pioneer even if he was still rather confused by all that was going on. It was a lot to process and understand all at once.

No turning back now, he thought.

"Today, I want to go back to a baseball game that my Dad brought me to when I was seven. My favorite moment I remember of my Dad from my childhood. I need a chill day, this time. A break from all of the chaos," said Louis.

Cody walked over from the other side of the virtual room. "That is your decision, Louie."

"Okay, cool."

Jack waved through the window on his way to his office. Louis waved back. When Jack was out of sight, Cody rolled his eyes.

"Bro, if you only knew what I knew, or seen what I've seen. You'd think a lot different about Mr. Jack, I can tell you that much. Like the time when…shit, never mind," said Cody as he started to type on his computer.

"You mean, because the dude just sits on his throne while the worker bees do everything to make this a better place? You guys are the ones that are changing the world," said Louis.

"Look, I'll put it like this," Cody said. "Jack has given me a career. He has done things for me no one else in the world ever did, or could do, at that. But I'd be lying if I said the dude didn't scare the shit out of me here and there. He's a mad scientist. But again, he gave me a life. A career. I get to be a part of something bigger than me and that is worth the sacrifice. That is worth doing what you gotta do, for the greater good," Cody explained.

"I understand, man," said Louis as he began to stretch his arms and legs to get ready for the next level.

Once he was all set up, Louis was transported back to the baseball game with his father when he was a child. He loved that day so much that he thought he would relive it the same exact way as the first time around. His Dad was particularly happy that day because he loved baseball more than nearly everything else.

To see that look on his father's face made it all worthwhile.

They went out to Malone's Frozen Yogurt after the game before going home to watch some scary movies together. Louis loved watching horror movies with his father before bed. It was a simpler time that made him feel back at home. It made him feel like a kid again.

Meanwhile, in real life, Cody was eating from a bowl of popcorn when he said to one of his fellow coders, "It's crazy how people really get sold on that nostalgia factor."

"Agreed," Mike, one of the other coders, replied.

"It's like people would rather relive a day like this, more than they could change any mistake they've ever made. It's fascinating to watch," said Cody as he jotted down notes and observed the game through the flat screen monitors. "Fascinating," he said again as he watched Louis, as a child, get tucked in by his father. It was a sweet moment for the coders to see, as well as especially useful information to analyze.

Chapter 12

The money was coming in steadily and Louis was taking care of everything he needed to. After taxes, he was clearing just over ten thousand dollars a week, more money than he knew what to do with.

"Louie!" yelled Jack as he cracked open a bottle of vodka. "You have been killing it during this trial run, my man."

"Thanks, Jack," he said as he stood up out of his seat.

"Cody has been keeping me informed of your progress and I must say...you have been exceeding all of our expectations, Lou. How about a drink?" he asked as he poured two shots of 100 proof Russian vodka. He handed one of the glasses to Louis and said, "Cheers, to you, Louie, and for all you are doing for us here at Mindtrick. Cheers."

"Cheers," Louis responded as they touched shot glasses before throwing them back. Louis made a face of disgust as he did not typically drink vodka, and this was top shelf.

"Lovely," said Jack as he poured himself another shot and took it. "Good shit, eh?" he asked as he wiped off the little that he got on his face. "Nothing like a bit of day drinking, am I right?" Jack took one more shot before he let out a righteous burp.

"I guess so," said Louis as he tried to get the taste of the strong liquor out of his mouth by taking a sip of his coffee. At that point, he preferred the taste of coffee.

"Hey Lou, you doing anything tonight? How about I take you out? We can grab some dinner, maybe hit up a club or something. C'mon, pal, what do ya say?"

Louis took a sip of his coffee and considered it. He thought about how he'd just gone partying with Roy in the game, but this was real life. Could he hang with his boss? He was not sure he wanted to say no, either. After a few moments, he looked at the clock on the wall and said, "Sure, Jack. Why the hell not?"

"Awesome, good shit. I'm excited, we haven't had a chance to get to know each other that much and you know, catch up. This will be good. Scratch that, this will be great. Gonna be a great night, Louie," said Jack as he sat down at his computer desk. "Let me make some calls and we'll leave at five on the dot."

"Sounds good," said Louis as he left Jack's office and went to check out what Cody and the team were up to.

"What's going on?" Louis asked.

"Not too much. Just working on some minor glitches in the gameplay," said Cody as he typed away.

"You're never gonna guess who just asked me to go out tonight."

Cody looked up from his computer screen. "Oh no, Jack con you into dinner and the club?"

"Yeah, how'd you know?" asked Louis.

"Man, dude used to always try to get me to go out with his crazy ass," Cody responded.

"Oh yeah?"

"Yeah, it was fun at first. Then I had to take a break from all of that. Jack can get...let's just say, he doesn't really have any limits, ya know?"

"What is he, some type of party animal or something?" asked Louis.

"That would be an understatement. The man is a genius, but once he has a little bit of booze or drugs in him, he can turn into somewhat of a monster, you catch my drift?" Cody said as he went back to typing on his computer.

"Ah shit, should I be concerned? Should I make something up and say I can't make it tonight?"

"Not if you already agreed to it. I mean, it isn't really that bad. I'm just saying, I've seen him go harder and get wilder than anyone in my life. My advice, go out, have fun. Have some good food, dance a little bit, but if things start to get weird or your gut is telling you something...call a cab and get the hell out of there. In fact, I would probably drive myself there just in case. If you let him drive, you might be stuck with him all night. He takes that wingman shit pretty serious," Cody explained. "And if you back out now, he's going to figure out I said something, and he already knows I don't get down like that anymore."

"Gotcha. All right, well, I'll keep my eyes open, I suppose," said Louis.

"Oh yeah, and do not…by any means, do not drink anything he gives you. Buy your own drinks. I've heard some despicable stories about him. Let's just say, he's been known to put stuff in people's drinks before. Not saying it's a fact or anything, but I've heard from more than one source. Just be careful, Louie," said Cody.

"Great. I just took a shot with him," said Louis.

"Oh no," said Cody as he typed into the company server.

"Now that I think about it, I saw him open the bottle. So, I think I should be all right," said Louis.

"Yeah, I'm probably just overthinking it. Forget I said anything. I'm just being paranoid. Don't know why but my trust for the man has crumbled exponentially over the years."

Just then, Jack walked by the room and snuck a peek at Cody, Louis, and the team.

"Speak of the devil," said Cody. "Act natural, laugh or something."

Louis started to laugh and kept cool like nothing was going on. Jack walked away.

"Gives you the creeps, huh?" said Cody.

"Not really. I'm a grown man, I can handle my own. But I guess he's a bit…eccentric, to say the least," Louis responded.

"Yeah, eccentric. That works, although it's being a tad generous if you ask me. If anything goes wrong while you guys are out, text me. But I'm sure you'll be okay. You got this, my dude," said Cody.

Later that night, Jack and Louis were sitting at a round golden table inside one of the most elegant, upscale restaurants around town, La Bella Cucina.

"How's that steak treating ya, big guy?" asked Jack.

"Gotta admit, this might be the best damn steak I've ever had," said Louis as he took another bite of the tender meat.

"Might? Shit, I'd have this for breakfast, lunch and dinner if I could," said Jack. "Matter of fact, I have. Midnight snack, too."

Louis started to laugh as he sipped his red wine. "The vino's not half bad, either," he said.

"Better be good, shit costs seven hundred dollars a bottle," said Jack as he chugged the rest of what he had in his glass. "But you're right, I suppose it could be better."

After dinner, Louis was stuffed as he sat at the table and listened to Jack ramble on with story after story, most of which ended with the same point of ultimately changing the world. He seemed a bit off, however, and his nose kept running. Louis got the feeling that his boss may have been under the influence of some sort of illegal substances. Jack was making it pretty obvious. He was talking non-stop and kept getting excited about everything.

Later, they found themselves at one of the hippest nightclubs in the city, Baewatch. It was more popular than ever since its grand opening the year prior. They sat in one of the roped-off VIP sections.

Electronic dance music thumped through the speakers, making it hard for Louis to hear himself think. Let alone hear what Jack was trying to yell to him.

"Can I ask you something, Louie?" yelled Jack as he took a shot of top-shelf cinnamon bourbon.

"Go for it."

"What did you want to be when you grew up?"

Louis took a swig from his beer bottle and thought to himself, *this dude is bat shit bananas.* Louis looked closely at Mr. Jack's face and could see a white powder under his nose. He knew he was in for a weird night. Jack started to make a funny face.

"I think I'm about to go number three in my pants!" said Jack.

"What's a number three?" asked Louis.

"You don't know, Louie? Piss and shit, man! Same time! When you go number one and number two at the same damn time, Lou!"

"Oh gross. Go use the bathroom, dude," said Louis.

"No, first answer my question. What did you want to be when you grew up?" asked Jack with a look of agony forming on his face as he tried to hold in his bowels and bladder.

Then Louis tried to come up with an answer his boss would accept. "Truth be told, I wanted to be an actor," he responded.

"What?" yelled Jack as he drank his Long Island iced tea.

"I said, I wanted to be an actor!" Louis reiterated as he finished up his beer.

Jack started cracking up. After laughing for a while, he responded, "That's funny. You're funny!"

"I need another drink. I'll be back!" said Louis as he started to get up from the red couch.

"This round is on me!" said Jack.

Louis thought back to what Cody told him earlier and replied, "No, it's cool. Lemme get this round. You've done so much for me. I insist. I'll get some shots, too!"

"That's my guy!" yelled Jack as he stood up and hugged Louis before he started to dance to the rhythm of the EDM song. The bass was blaring through the club speakers so loud it made Louis' beard vibrate. The song playing was a new remix of a track that was currently all over the radio and on top of the charts. It was called "Way Late" by Starstruck. The remix came out that month. Jack appeared to be a big fan of the track. Louis could tell when he flared his arms in the air. He danced like nobody was watching. When in fact, a few people were watching. One even began to film it on his phone. Jack did not care as he stuck his tongue out for the camera and made the devil horns hand sign over his head. Then he began to dance around the people who were laughing at him until they walked away.

Louis got to the bar and waited in line. He looked back and saw Jack dancing his heart out and began to laugh. He started to think, *maybe this guy isn't that bad after all.* Then Jack looked over at Louis, made a face, and ran to the bathroom at full speed.

Later, they were outside having a smoke when Louis looked at his phone and noticed it was almost midnight. He was exhausted, but he did not want that to show. He was trying to impress Jack. He knew he had a good thing going and did not want to ruin it in any way, shape, or form.

"You having fun, Louie?" asked Jack as he took a puff from the cigarette Louis gave him.

"Actually, I really am," he responded.

"I'm glad to hear, bud," said Jack.

"I'm not really the dancing type; I don't go out that much."

"No shit, really?" said Jack sarcastically.

Louis laughed, "Yeah, sorry, I'm sure that's pretty obvious." Louis inhaled the smoke from his cigarette.

He looked up at the stars that filled the night sky like brightly lit chicken pox.

"It's cool, honestly, Louie..." Jack said as he began to slur his words a bit. "I wouldn't be here either, if I didn't own a third of the club."

"You're kidding me, really?"

"You bet," said his boss as he finished his cigarette and tossed it out on to the sidewalk.

"That's freaking nuts," said Louis as he flicked his cigarette into the street.

"You know, Louie. You know, I know it seems like I have this sort of spiritual view of life as we know it. But really, I'm just like anyone else, I don't really know shit.

I'm just damn good at developing videogames. Can you believe my mother told me I'd never amount to anything playing games all the time? Now look at me," said Jack.

"You're an impressive man, Mr. Jack," said Louis.

"If you're still trying to party, I can make a text and have some beautiful ladies meet us on the dance floor. Trust me, Lou, you won't be disappointed."

Louis let out a yawn and then slapped himself before he said, "Screw it, let's live it up. Or like my daughter says, let's turn up. Or turn this up. No, turn up. That's it."

Jack started to laugh and grabbed Louis by the shoulders. "Turn up!" he yelled as he pulled out his smartphone to text his business associate.

As they made their way back inside, Jack said to Louis, "Just don't make a fool out of me in front of the ladies. Kinda like Cody did one time. Scared off these fine females we were talking to. Guy can code, but the only girl he can get would have to be a sex doll. The kid has zero game. Pun intended."

"No problem. I'll try my best. I mean…I'll be cool," said Louis as he followed Jack in the direction of the music. They reached the dance floor to find four beautiful women in the front waving to them.

"Meet my friend, Louis!" Jack yelled to the ladies.

"Hey Louie!" the four said at the same time. Two of them walked up and kissed both of his cheeks simultaneously.

"Be nice to my friend," said Jack as he told a nearby waitress to bring them a round of shots and mixed drinks. He also ordered Louis another beer, only after whispering special instructions into the shot girl's ear. She nodded and smiled.

They got their drinks and Jack proceeded to make a toast: "To my main guy, Louie!"

They all clinked shots together and then took them in unison. Louis grabbed his beer and started to chug it to get the taste of the bitter liquor out of his mouth. As the beer went down, he began to feel a little funny. He was already exhausted. He continued to drink his beer as two of the girls, Molly and Lucy, danced with him.

After a few songs, Molly sat on his lap and started making out with Louis. He was feeling good, as all his inhibitions flew right out of the window. He kissed her back, until Lucy pulled her off him and kissed him as well. Then the two girls moved on to French kissing each other. Louis started dancing and getting into it when he looked over at his boss who had a gigantic smile on his face.

"Louie! You only live once! Maybe next trial day you can relive tonight!" Jack yelled as he danced with the other two women. Louis' vision blurred and he felt a little dizzy. He wobbled back and forth before dropping down to the ground like a sack of potatoes.

When Louis woke up in his own bed, he had no recollection of what had happened to him. All he remembered was going out to eat with Jack and meeting girls at a night club after. The rest of the night became a blur. Louis jumped up out of bed, ran to his bathroom and puked in the toilet.

Days went by and it was time for Louis to play *Seven Days VR* once again. This time, Louis wanted to pick a somewhat subtle day, but one that had a big impact on his life. He decided to pick the day he failed one of his big finals in his second year of college. That ultimately led to him losing faith in himself and dropping out of school completely. He never went back to finish his degree. He always wondered what his life would have been like had he passed that test and that class. He never thought he would have the opportunity to do it over. Then again, he never really wanted to, either.

Once Louis realized that was the day he wanted to relive, he went online to study college algebra and bring himself up to speed on what the test would cover. Since it was a final, it basically went over everything from the beginning of the semester. Louis studied as much as he could before Day Six of the trial run. He felt like he was as ready as he would ever be.

Cody and the team sat back and watched as Louis was virtually teleported to his sophomore year at Monroe State College.

He then had a long and grueling test that took him just under two hours to finish.

Louis waited around the school after the test. He wanted to find out how he did. Before the level was finished the next day, Louis went to his teacher's classroom to ask her if he could get his grade for the test. He made up an excuse about going on vacation so he could get his score early. His teacher obliged and put his test through the grading machine. After waiting twenty minutes, she came out of her office with his test in hand. He had passed with a score of 82.

He celebrated in the school hallway by jumping up in the air and clicking his basketball shoes together as he always knew he could pass if he applied himself and actually studied. Then, he got a little depressed when he thought about how none of this was real. And when he went back to reality, he'd still be a college dropout. He wished there were some way passing that test and staying in school could be permanent.

There were only a couple hours left in the level. Then out of nowhere, the lights and computers throughout the Mindtrick games building all shut on and off multiple times until the lights stayed off. The monitors went blank.

"What the hell?" asked Cody.

Another coder said, "The system's down, the Wi-Fi, too. Louis might be stuck in there for a while."

"Well, what the shit are we standing around for? We gotta get the system booted back up!" Cody shouted as he ran around in the dark looking for the backup breaker on the wall. He found it and flipped it up and down. But nothing happened.

Back in the game, Louis walked aimlessly, wondering if the level would ever come to an end. After hours upon hours, he figured he would go to a college party and hang out for a bit until the game was over.

At the party, Louis ended up getting totally hammered until he passed out on the front lawn of the fraternity house. He made his way back to his dorm room. Days turned to weeks as he finished his college semester. He finally went back home for summer break.

After a few months, he finally forgot he was in a game at all. He thought he was living his normal life. And just like that, he was transported back to real life through the quantum game realm and Level Six was in the books. The power and the Wi-Fi in the building were only out for twenty minutes, but in the game, it felt like half a year had passed.

The power of the game was unprecedented, and there was no real way of measuring time elapsed in the game versus real life. Cody thought the ratio might be different for everyone. For Louis, it seemed as if time slowed down to the fullest while the internet was down. But for some others, time could speed faster than in real life. Cody hoped that sort of thing would not happen often. But when it did, there would need to be a protocol set in place on what to do. Cody was just happy that Louis finally regained consciousness.

When Louis opened his eyes, he had no idea where he was. He forgot he worked for Mindtrick Games. It took hours for everything to come back to him.

"Can we order that backup generator already?" asked Cody as he ran tests on Louis to make sure there was no permanent damage done to his brain.

Chapter 13

Louis sat outside of his apartment on a bench where he lit a cigarette and watched the clouds move slowly through the sky. One peculiar shaped cloud collided with a bigger cloud of a similar shape becoming one giant cloud. He let out his own cloud of smoke before tossing his cigarette.

He got up off the bench and stepped on the cigarette burning down to the butt. Then, Louis walked into his apartment lobby and waved to Bob, who ran the front desk during the day shift.

"Never change, Bob!" yelled Louis.

"Wouldn't even if I could," Bob said.

"You're the man," said Louis as he headed up the stairs back to his studio that he had been upgrading lately.

Once inside, Louis plopped on his couch and reflected on everything he had been doing. It felt great most of the time, but he also had a little bit of regret that he had the ability to live in the past. He was always told by his father to never live in the past. This experience did not support that saying, as living in the past was quite awesome, especially in Virtual Reality form. At least that's how it felt to Louis so far.

The next day, Louis met with Cody in the Mindtrick Games office secondary lab. They were going over the results from his last trial run.

"Can I ask you something?" asked Louis.

"Shoot," Cody responded.

"How did you guys come up with the name, *Seven Days in Virtual Reality?*"

"Actually, that was all Jack. Yeah, I don't know really. I guess it makes sense and goes with the overall theme of the game, ya know?" said Cody.

"Right. I mean, sure there is definitely some religious symbolism when you think about it," said Louis.

"Yeah, also… deep down I genuinely think that Jack thinks that he is…well…God. He surely walks around like his shit don't stink most days. And I've been in the bathroom after him, and his shit stinks," said Cody before bursting out laughing.

"Good one," said Louis. "That's what us Dads would call a Dad joke. You'd be a good Dad, Cody."

"Thanks, Louis," Cody said as he continued to laugh.

"It is the most rewarding thing in the world, my dude. Trust me. My kids are the best. Even at their worst."

"I believe it, Louis. I'm sure they're great kids. So, where are we going for your final day in the trial?" asked Cody as he hooked up the VR console.

"You know, I always regretted not having a crazy bachelor party. I chickened out at the last minute and went home early. My friends had a killer night planned for me and I just blew them off like a jackass. So, yeah... let's go back then."

"Alrighty," said Cody as he finished starting up the system.

Louis thought for a second and then said, "Hey Cody, what happens after this? Am I done? You think I'll get to stay at Mindtrick? I gotta admit, I kinda like it here."

"You know, that's not up to me. But if it were, I'd love to have you here for the long run," said Cody.

"Thank you, my friend," said Louis. He was flattered. He thought this was by far the coolest thing he had ever been a part of, and he wanted to stay. As long as he was welcome.

"Well, we may have another job for you. Not sure just yet. But Jack has mentioned something about needing a tester for Version Two which we only recently finalized. I shouldn't say anything else, but if I'm right then Jack might offer you another position once this is all over."

"Damn, I hope so," said Louis.

The team finished setting Louis up in his equipment. Cody punched in the date: April 4, 2004. A month before Louis married his now ex-wife, Denise.

As Louis was loading into the game, Jack walked into the virtual room.

"Cody how are things looking?" he asked as he drank from his go-to black and red coffee mug.

"Everything's looking good for the most part," said Cody, as he watched the game load on the large, flat screen high definition 6K monitor.

Jack obviously had something on his mind. "Listen," Jack began. "I've been thinking about it. And I'm starting to come to the conclusion that Louis would really be great for the Version Two trials. If he's all right with it, of course, once he recharges after a month of playing *Seven Days*. I honestly think we'll get much better results if we test that beta out, as well. Don't get me wrong. The original is great. It is a masterpiece. But Version Two. Cody, you, and I both know the potential in Version Two. I say we give the guy the option and if he decides to stay…then great. If not, we can find someone else when the time is right. You catch my drift, Cody?" said the founder with a sketchy look in his eye.

"Jack, listen, with all due respect, I really think we need a moment to process all of the results from Version One and analyze the first game that we've dedicated the last three years to developing. Sir."

"Like I said, if he wants to stay on, then that's that. I'm not forcing anyone's hand here, Cody."

"I get that," said the master coder as he watched the game finish loading.

Louis was transported virtually to the bar where his bachelor party was taking place. Cody continued, "It's your call, Jack. This is your game. All we do is code it. Whatever you say, goes."

In the game, Louis was out raging with some of his best friends, and with his two brothers whom he did not usually spend a lot of quality time with. He remembered the day like it was yesterday. But this time, instead of going home early, he stayed out and drank with his bachelor crew while they hopped from bar to bar before ending up at the strip club.

One thing led to another as the boys continued to rag until the early morning. Louis' brother, Roy, gave the bachelor a powerful painkiller after one too many shots. Louis did not stop and continued to party until the point of no return. Finally, around 2 a.m., Louis lost consciousness and fell down to the ground, slamming his head against the corner of the table they were sitting at. Blood surrounded his head and then his body to the point where his friends started to panic. Roy pulled out his cell phone and called the police. An hour later, Louis was pronounced dead in the club.

The game ended abruptly, and the team ran over to take off the equipment. Jack and Cody watched and could not believe what they had just witnessed. Then Louis came to.

"Holy shit!" he yelled as he opened his eyes and looked around the room. "Did I die?"

"You did," said Jack, still in disbelief.

"I saw a black light, and then…a white light! It was stunning. Looked and felt like I was being teleported through a tunnel somewhere or some shit. And then, I was back here," said Louis as he could barely tell where he was.

"That was quite an epic way to go out," said Jack as he started to clap his hands.

Cody walked over to Louis and shined a flashlight into his eyes to examine him. They had not designed a protocol to use if someone died in the game. He was not sure what to do. He had no clue what harm could have been done. Cody decided he had many tests to run on Louis to make sure that he was all right, and to mitigate any possible damage.

Hours later, Cody went back to check on Louis in the Infirmary and to ask him a few questions.

"How are you feeling?"

"I've been worse, I suppose," said Louis.

"Any major side effects I should know about? Aside from the obvious headaches, migraines, body aches, and whatnot?" asked Cody.

"Well…I hear this constant ringing in my ear, and it gets louder and louder until it becomes a sharp piercing echo. Should I be concerned?" asked Louis with a worried look on his face. "It kinda hurts, but I can manage."

"No. That's normal. I meant more like have you started pissing blood… or anything of that nature? That was one thing we were scared might happen," said Cody.

"No?" Louis replied with a quick look down at his privates.

"Okay good. And don't worry. That ringing in your ears will go away," said Cody.

"Oh yeah? When's that?" asked Louis.

"Most likely in one to five years or so," Cody responded.

"You've got to be kidding!"

"That was cool as shit!" Jack interrupted as he walked over to Louis and shook his hand. "You've done us proud, here at Mindtrick...Louie, you're the man."

After he got discharged, Louis dressed and then walked down the long hallway toward the lobby.

Jack was waiting at the front door and took Louis aside. "Here, Louie," Jack said, handing him an envelope. "Just a small bonus for doing such a great job testing my game," said Jack. Then he hugged Louis tight.

"It has been an honor, Jack," Louis said as he hugged him back. "I hope I get to work with you guys again. You know, once the seven days are done."

"Yes. Well, so. Louie, I may, or may not...but I may have another position for you lined up."

"No way. I mean, oh really. Go on," said Louis.

"Okay. Here, let me explain. So, *Seven Days VR* is much more than just the one game that you tested for us.

That was simply Version One. But there is a second version that we've just moved into beta phase. It's—shall we say—a bit more advanced. It's for serious gamers that want to take it to the next level. It is pretty much the same concept as the one you played, with a few tiny differences.

"The main distinction is that when you leave the second version of the game...how do I put it...well, when you come back to reality, the outcomes of your actions are permanent. I know, I know. It sounds crazy. Sure. But we didn't think the experience of just reliving the day was enough. There are people that want to change their past. And we have figured out a way to make that happen for our users. This quantum technology is years upon years ahead of its time. But if we can prove its worth and use, it could be like a subscription-based program. And only our best and most serious players will get to use it.

"This version, Version Two...is the real game-changer. This one will for sure change the world in ways that the first version simply cannot. Because in the end, Version One is just a game. This is the real deal. This one has consequences. For instance, if you die in Version Two, you die in real life. Which means your decisions carry that much more weight.

"Anyway, not trying to hold you up. Go home, get some rest. I will see you for analysis tomorrow. We'll talk more. Again, great job, Lou," said Jack as he patted him on the back and walked away.

Louis did not know what to think. He turned around and walked away, speechless. He looked in his envelope to find a check for twenty thousand dollars. He realized he'd just been handed almost half the amount he'd expected for the entire job. He could not believe his good fortune. In his eyes, he was becoming rich.

On the way home that night, Louis stopped at his favorite megastore, Yalmarket's, to pick up a few things for the house. While he was there, he grabbed a case of Mudringer light beer.

Later that night he would finish a third of the beer. Before he fell asleep, he could not help but wonder what Jack was talking about with Version Two. Could that even be possible? He looked around at his new, big screen, high-definition TV and his new furniture and realized he had something pretty good going. He decided that whatever

Jack would offer him, he was ready, willing, and able to do it. He was hooked. Louis smiled, closed his eyes, and fell asleep.

Chapter 14

Louis was not quite sure if he had made the right decision to test out the second version of the game. But he was blinded by the money. He could not get enough. In his mind, it was a fortune. At first, he thought he would live off of the fifty thousand dollars he'd made for at least a year until he decided where to go next. But once the option to keep working for Mindtrick arose, he could not turn it down. Between the starting bonus, monthly fee, and end bonus, he had already grossed eighty thousand dollars. He wondered what Jack would offer him to test the second version of the game.

There were a few moments of doubt where he thought he should probably walk away while he still could. Maybe he was getting himself into something dangerous. He'd started hearing rumors about Jack. He heard that Jack was going to use the new games to steal people's memories and sell them for profit to the highest bidding mobile tech giant. He also heard that Jack might be using the company as one giant drug front. Maybe he should get out while things were still good, before they could turn ugly. Then again, he was also enjoying the ride. He was doing things he never thought imaginable, let alone possible.

Louis felt fine after the first set of trials of *Seven Days VR* was over, except for a couple of minor side effects, such as lucid dreams, and chronic insomnia. He also had minor damage to his overall eyesight caused by his extended time spent in virtual reality. His eyes would slowly adjust to the console's picture settings, and it was hard at times for him to transition back to reality. Especially considering the number of hours each day that testing entailed. But he soon became used to that part, and almost had a craving for that feeling as the tests went on.

However, he found he enjoyed being in the virtual world more than real life once he got the hang of it. By the time he really grasped the game itself, the trial was already complete. Louis knew that he never had good timing when it came to leaving the casino while he was still up. *And, yet,* he thought. *I managed Version One just fine. How hard could Version Two really be?*

"Are you absolutely sure you're cool with this?" asked Cody as he turned on some monitors to prep the virtual lab. "I'm just saying, the first version was easy, in comparison. This one…this one might take a little bit more out of you, you know?"

"I think I can handle it, bud," said Louis as he drank his coffee. "Unless should I be worried? You seem on edge today, Cody," he said as he put his coffee cup down on the table. "Is there something else?"

"No. It's fine. Just forget it. Sorry, I had a rough night. Don't mind me," said Cody as he turned on the consoles and rechecked the equipment. "I was just saying, this version of the game is a bit harder, that's all."

"Brother, for this kind of money, there is truly very little that I would not do. Playing a cool new videogame doesn't sound too bad. Plus, I got it down. I think I'll do even better this time," Louis said.

"I'm sure you will, Louie," said Cody before he went over and printed out copies of a report from their last session. "I know you'll do great. You're a company man, I get that."

On his way home from work, Louis stopped at Paul's Diner and picked up a few meals to eat by himself when he was back home. After he got the bag of food in the car, he put it in the passenger seat and buckled it in with the seat belt. He did this from time to time to make sure that the food did not fly around the car or spill all over the seats.

That night, Louis was tossing and turning in his sleep. He was having a dream about *Seven Days in Virtual Reality*.

In the dream, Louis was strapped into his headset, playing the game. Except everything felt distorted, different than it felt in real life.

At first it was adventurous and fun, until he got to a memory in which he and his old friend from childhood, Kyler, were on a small airplane getting ready to go skydiving.

This terrified Louis because he had always been afraid of heights. First, Kyler jumped out of the side of the plane. On his way out he screamed, "See ya at the bottom, Lou!" He stuck his tongue out and threw up the devil horns hand sign like a rock star floating through the sky. Louis watched him as he soared, flipping through the clouds, until he was the size of an ant.

Louis did not want to jump, but something inside of him was telling him to ignore his instincts and leap from the plane. At first, Louis resisted. Then he heard a whisper in his ear from a familiar voice that said, "Jump." This spooked Louis, as he turned around and no one was there. He assumed that his conscious was trying to tell him something. Then, the voice spoke in his ear again: "Jump."

Louis tried not to look down too much as he began to panic. He heard the voice in his ear one more time before he turned around. Just then, a man's shadowy figure shoved him so hard that before he knew it, Louis was out of the plane and darting through the sky, piercing the air on his way down. When he looked back up at the plane, the man faintly resembled Mr. Jack. He was sporting a huge grin across his face. Louis free-fell from what felt like tens of thousands of feet. He could see the ground getting closer and closer.

The fall felt like it would last forever as the clouds continued to pass Louis on his way down.

Louis attempted to pull the latch to open his parachute, but nothing happened. In a panic, Louis pulled and pulled as he continued falling. When he got about a hundred feet from the ground, the parachute opened. But it was too late and did not totally stop his fall.

When Louis crashed, he heard his whole lower body crack and snap. As he lay there, he realized he couldn't move and started becoming frantic.

Finally, he woke up and realized it was all a dream. Louis leapt out of his bed to make sure he could still feel his legs. He stumbled to the bathroom and looked at himself in the mirror. He could not remember a dream ever feeling that real in his whole life.

Louis walked over to his kitchen and chugged a glass of chilled water. Then he took a few deep breaths, as he thanked the lord his nightmare was over. Now he just wondered how in the world he would ever get back to sleep.

Chapter 15

It was Louis' last day at work for his testing of Version One. Cody and the team had completed all the tests and procedural duties with Louis before thanking him for his work. Then, at Jack's request, Cody sent Louis to Jack's office for a final meeting.

Louis knocked on the door as it opened slowly. He found Jack working at his computer. Jack quickly turned his screen away so Louis could not see what he was doing before standing up and shouting, "Louie!"

"Cody told me to come see you."

"Right. Looks like our time has come," said Jack as he fixed his tie and rolled up his sleeves. "Take a seat."

Louis sat down and watched his boss walk around the room. "Again, I want to thank you so much for the opportunity."

Jack cut him off, "Louie, Louie…Lou, my man. Just, I don't know. I hate to see you go. I would hate to see you leave us, man. I think you're a great fit here at Mindtrick."

"Much appreciated," said Louis.

"I'm going to cut to the chase. I don't want to find somebody else for this job. I want you. You passed Version One and beat the game with flying colors. You don't have to decide right away, of course. Well, actually you sort of do. I'll let you sleep on it at least. But if you do want to stay with us, I can offer you one hundred thousand dollars for your contributions. You deserve good money for good work," said the CEO.

Louis could not believe it. He was at a loss for words. That was a lot of money. More than he could even imagine. He started to consider the fact that he would not have to work for at least a few months, maybe even another year or two, with that kind of money. He could move to a bigger apartment. Pay off all his credit card debt. Buy a new car. Buy Natalie a car. Get Tommy tutors so he had a better chance of getting into a good college. He was stunned, frozen in place for a moment.

"That's… a lot of money, Jack."

"Well, it's a harder game, Louie," he said as he took a sip from his coffee. "If you take the job, you gotta take it very seriously. The repercussions of your actions could be grand. I mean, in comparison to the original, Version Two of *Seven Days VR* has the potential to transcend more than just the world of videogames."

"But will it change the world?" asked Louis. He knew that he wanted the job but did not want to appear too desperate either. He thought for a second and said, "I'm going to have to think about it."

"Understandable. Think about it, my man," said Jack.

"It's been an honor, seriously," said Louis.

"Likewise, bud." Jack walked over to show him out of his office. "Gimme a call and let me know what we're doing, Louie. But I need your answer in twenty-four hours or I will immediately start my search for a new tester."

"Will do," he said as he walked out.

But Jack knew Louis would probably be back, and so did Louis.

Louis awoke from a bad dream that he was running away from Jack with a wire connecting them to one another. The dream finally ended when Louis ran off a cliff to escape his boss and only woke up moments before he hit the ground. He could not stop having dreams that ended in him falling. Many times, falling to his death. He wondered if his dreams were trying to tell him something or if they were portents of his future.

Holy shit. That was terrifying, he said to himself as he sat up and got out of bed to use the bathroom.

He stared at himself in the mirror and leaned on the counter. Then he turned on the cold water and splashed a little bit on his face. Perhaps it was just a terrible dream with no meaning at all.

The clock struck 4 a.m. Louis could not get himself back to sleep once he started thinking about the new job. He thought about all the money he would make, and how he'd be set for a long time.

He picked up his phone and sent a text to Jack's personal cell phone. "I accept the new job. Version Two it is," Louis wrote.

"Wise choice," Jack responded a few minutes later.

Louis was amazed his boss was also awake at 4 a.m. Or maybe he had not gotten to sleep yet.

A couple of weeks went by before Louis was scheduled to come in for training for *Seven Days in Virtual Reality*, Version Two. Fortunately, the ringing in his ears and the occasional migraines had already gone away. He felt ready and eager to test out Version Two. He felt like the chosen one again. He had no clue what to expect, but at least he was more ready than the first time around.

He sat at the table with the team of coders as Jack went over a few things. Cody sat next to him with his notepad in one hand and tablet in the other.

"We will spend a week training for Version Two, just like we did for Version One," Cody said. "The training is a bit more intensive. You will need to lend even more focus and energy this time around. But I have faith you can do it," Cody explained. "We all have faith in you."

He wrote an equation on the chalkboard that looked like transmissions from an intergalactic race from an earth-like exoplanet. Then he continued with rows of algebra.

Louis could not even begin to comprehend this next-level math.

"Lou don't worry about that. That stuff on the board is for the team. It's the key to the entire algorithm that makes this beta work. Much different than the other software's codes. You just worry about being your best self, we'll handle all the complicated shit."

"Got it," said Louis. He had no clue what it meant but wrote it in his notebook anyway:

$$(17ub)/3 + 5vb - e = R \times 7M$$

"You will have to make much more conscious and collected decisions this time, so it's important that you remain calm and not let your emotions get the best of you. Because what happens in the game will have side effects and chain reactions in real life. *High tide*. You must remember that Lou."

"Right," said Louis as he became more and more confused. He was not sure if he was even hearing Cody clearly/correctly.

"Cool. So, this part is particularly important. You must be safe, very safe. You cannot risk your life, like you could during your first trial run. If you get hurt, or at worst, die…you cannot come back. The consequences are real. I cannot stress that enough, Louie," said Cody.

"I gotcha," said Louis. But his insomnia was affecting his concentration, so he was still a bit lost. All he pretty much understood was to try not to die. Seemed simple enough.

"Okay, good. Don't get me wrong. You still have free will. And you are ultimately the one who decides everything you do in the game. All I can do is warn you. Version Two is no joke, Louie," Cody said.

He wrote some more code on the chalkboard. The team sat and listened. Most of them already knew everything they were hearing but they still watched Cody do his presentation.

"Got it, not a joke. Noted," said Louis as he jotted in his notebook.

Then Cody wrote an interesting quote on the board in capital letters. It read:

DON'T LET YOUR PAST DESTROY YOUR FUTURE.

"I know it sounds like some inspirational bullshit, but it is one hundred percent legit," said Cody. "Even if it does sound corny as hell."

"It's cool. I'll write that down," said Louis as he dutifully copied it into his notebook. "They can even put that on my tombstone, I like that."

Cody laughed. "Great, dude. Oh yeah. So. This one is different in many ways, but specifically the first two levels. They are combined. It was the only way for the game to work the way it does. But just the first two. Then there are breaks between the rest of the levels," Cody explained as he and the rest of the team began to set up the updated console.

"Whatever's clever," said Louis. He craved a cigarette. He looked in his pockets to see if he had any left in his pack. But he could not find them. He started to panic, checking his pockets for his cigarettes. He thought he had lost them. Then he checked his back pocket, and there they were. *Phew*, he said to himself.

"I'm gonna go have a smoke, guys. I'll be back in five," Louis said as he made his way out of the virtual lab.

The week went by excruciatingly slowly. Louis tried to take everything in as he trained for Version Two of *Seven Days*.

Cody could only help him so much. He emphasized that once the game started, it could not be paused or stopped. Louis would have to complete the day/level he was experiencing before he would be able to go back to reality. It was all a bit much for Louis to understand, but he thought he got the gist of it.

Over the weekend, Louis had Natalie and Tommy over at his brand new four thousand-square foot co-op townhouse in the nicer side of town. The house had four bedrooms and three bathrooms, as well as a two-car garage. He was looking at new cars that he planned on purchasing to fill his new garage. He bought both kids brand new smartphones and started savings accounts for each of them. His kids were happy that their father seemed to be doing better financially, especially when he bought them nice things.

It was Sunday, the night before he would begin testing the new game. He had been working out more than ever, to prepare himself physically for the new position. Louis also started doing yoga, which Cody recommended to him. He said it would help him keep a grip on reality, as well as virtual reality. Cody seemed afraid he might start to confuse the two after a while, working at Mindtrick for too long.

"Hey Dad. I'm hungry," said Tommy.

"Well hello hungry, I'm Dad," said Louis.

"Okay, that one was terrible," Tommy replied.

"Your sister thought it was hilarious."

"I doubt that, but even if she did…she's a buffoon."

"Don't call her that. If she's a buffoon, you're a buffoon by relation!" Louis exclaimed.

"Listen Dad, do you think I can get a car for my birthday?" asked Tommy as he scrolled down his phone looking at pictures on social media.

"But you're only turning sixteen?"

"I just have to be fifteen and a half to get a driver's permit."

"But do you think you deserve a car, son?" asked Louis as he cooked elbow pasta with his special homemade sauce.

"Well…yeah, I mean. I don't do anything bad," said Tommy.

"Let me think about it," said his father as he tasted the sauce and then continued to stir it. "Nice," he said."

Natalie walked over to Louis and showed him a picture of her report card and said, "Boom!"

"Wow, straight A's," said Louis. "See, Tommy, this is what I want to see!" he said as he hugged and kissed his daughter.

"Get out of here, Natalie. No one cares," said Tommy.

"Jealous much?" she said as she walked away.

"Look, Tom. How about this? You come over here and mow my lawn every other week, as well as get your grades up, and I'll think about getting you a really nice previously owned car. How does that sound?" said Louis as he put his pasta in the strainer.

"Deal," said Tommy as he started to play the mobile game, Party Monsters, on his new phone. "By the way, dinner smells good."

"Thanks Tommy," said Louis.

"You know, Dad. Maybe one day you can get me a job at Mindtrick games. Looks like you're going to be there for a while."

Louis thought for a second and said, "We'll see, son. If all goes well and I end up staying there for a while, sure, why the hell not? I can ask about getting you a job interview there."

"Awesome," said Tommy as he walked over to the beautiful large kitchen he was not used to seeing when he visited his Dad every other weekend.

The sun began to rise as light projected through the blinds of Louis' master bedroom. His new townhouse was painted yellow and white and had lots of space left inside since Louis was still getting settled in. He also needed to buy some new furniture and other household items. The only groceries he had were the ones he used to make dinner the night before. He had to get his life at his new home in order. But today, he had work, and his new position called for a lot of focus and dedication. He had been meditating in preparation.

He finally woke up, just after 7 a.m. He got out of bed and freshened up for the day that lay ahead. He had an eerie feeling that things were going to get weird.

He dropped his kids off at Denise's house, his old house, and headed to work.

Louis was a few blocks away from the office, a half hour before the workday would begin. He was a bit nervous, so he lit a cigarette. He noticed it was the last one of the pack and decided to stop at the corner store across the street from his office's parking lot.

He walked inside just as a woman in a red dress was walking out. They bumped into each other on the other side of the doorway inside the store. "Pardon me," said Louis.

"It's all right," she said.

She was quite stunning to him and he could not help himself from saying, "My name is Louis."

"Oh, cool." She looked at her phone and said, "Look Louis, I'm sorry but…I have a boyfriend."

Embarrassed and defeated, Louis backed up and said, "My bad. He's a lucky guy," before walking to the back of the store to grab a drink.

She left, and he went up to the cashier. "Pack of Bearstick Menthol 100s please," Louis said as he handed over a twenty-dollar bill. Keep the change," he exclaimed before walking out of the front door.

On his way out, the store clerk yelled, "Thank you, my friend!"

Louis walked by the front desk in the Mindtrick Games lobby and said, "Hey Emily." She looked up at him with a smile.

"Good morning, Mr. Parker," she said as she eyed him up and down.

"Good morning, Emily," he replied as he walked away.

"Glad you're still here," she said as he got further away. He turned around and went to speak to her when he noticed she was gone. It was like she just vanished into thin air. One minute she was there, the next moment she was gone. It almost felt like she was some sort of augmented reality being for a moment.

That's weird, he thought to himself.

He turned around to walk to Jack's office when he was startled to find Emily right behind him. "You look good, Louis Parker," she said as she hugged him and kissed him on the cheek. "Mr. Jack has given me special orders to serve you in any way I can."

"Umm, wow, that's great...Emily. Umm, I got to go find Jack actually. So, I'll...talk to you later," he said as he walked away, blushing.

Then he turned back around, and she was already sitting at the front desk in her rolling chair.

The phone rang and she answered it.

"Mindtrick Games. This is Emily," she said as she looked over at Louis and gave him a quick wink. He winked back and continued walking.

Louis met Cody, Jack, and an even larger team of coders in the massive virtual room. When he walked in, they gave him a round of applause, as per Jack's specific orders. Louis felt a warm welcome from the team. "Thank you, you guys are too kind," he said as he shook everyone's hand. He gave Cody a hug. Then another hug to Jack.

"My man. My main man!" said Jack. "Here to change the world, again!"

All the training had slowly turned into one big blur. But Louis figured he would just go with the flow. It worked for him the first time. He probably should have studied the manual and books he received over the last week. But either way, he trusted Cody to look out for him in case anything went wrong. But Louis did not think it would. The first time was fine. He came out unscathed and ready for more.

The first day of trials for beta Version Two of *Seven Days VR* was now officially underway. Cody and the team were getting the virtual room all set up to begin. This time, Louis would have to do a more extensive upload process, as well as have a chip implanted in his brain. This procedure was for added graphics, effects and to help them track his progress better, physically and mentally. They also had him swallow what they described as vitamins. One of them contained a tracker, while another one was a Redtooth wireless connection feature. It was part of the tech that made the second version work smoothly with the quantum database. It was extremely complicated and had to be executed to perfection to get the desired results.

Louis went to the locker room to change into more appropriate clothes. He noticed he had a text message from Tommy. It read, "Good luck at work, Dad. I love you."

He smiled and texted back, "Love you too, son. Thanks a lot."

He shut off his phone and changed into his neon yellow and black jumpsuit before heading back to the virtual room.

They were ready to begin testing as Louis prepared for the upload procedure. He remembered it hurt like hell the first time. Fortunately, for this upload, he did not feel as much pain; he thought that maybe he had built up a slight tolerance since he started working there. It lasted twice as long as the first time, with Louis sending every memory and thought his brain contained through wires into the game's system where they were saved as terabytes of metadata in the Mindtrick server. If Louis had read the entire terms and conditions agreement, he would have known that his memories were now owned and licensed by the Mindtrick Corporation to be used as they saw fit.

It was over. Louis had a small migraine, but they told him that would subside shortly. A team member brought him a glass of water. Cody worked on his laptop for a while before saying, "Whenever you're ready, Louie...we can begin the game."

"Let's go," said Louis as he chugged the ice-cold water. He stretched a bit and did some push-ups before he let the team put on his gear.

This time, he had a larger VR headset. And instead of the controller gloves, they helped him slip on a slick-looking high-tech body suit with lights glistening from top to bottom. "Whoa, I feel like a superhero or whatever, I don't know...is this what my son calls a skin?" Louis asked as he wiggled around in the suit until it fit nice and snug.

"Well, your skin is what you wear in the game. But yeah, Louie, you do look like a superhero," said Cody as he typed on his computer.

Then, Cody inserted the game disc into the console and *Seven Days VR*, Version Two, began to load.

"Sweet," said Louis as the team placed the new headset on his head and strapped it in place. Louis could feel his palms sweat as he braced for whatever was about to happen next.

"Where are we going first?" asked Cody.

"Well, I remember what you said about being safe this time, so for the first level...let's go to Halloween night when I was...nine. Wait, I mean ten. Let me get a little bit more used to this version of the game."

"You got it, Louie."

Cody looked up keywords "Halloween" and "age ten", and the memory came up. "Got it, ready whenever you are," he said.

Louis had a moment of doubt, then he snapped out of it when he remembered how much money was coming his way. "Ready," he said as he took a deep breath. He began to count backwards from ten. "Ten. Nine. Eight. Seven. Six. Five...."

Cody pushed "Enter" and the game was launched. Jack walked into the virtual room and watched as Louis transported to Halloween night, 1990. The game loaded for thirty seconds before the level began.

Louis spawned on a street near his childhood home. He was with his two friends, Miles and Rodney. He looked down and saw he was dressed like a zombie. His friends were both vampires.

"I hope we get some good candy!" said Miles.

"We will," said Rodney.

"Then we can use these once the candy situation is taken care of," said Miles as he opened his backpack to reveal three cartons of eggs.

"Oh snap!" said Rodney.

"What do you think, Louis?" asked Miles

Amazed at the clarity and detail of this second version of the game, Louis looked at his childhood friend and said, "Gonna be sweet!" in his innocent child voice. He looked in the window of a car that they passed and could not believe what he saw in his reflection. He was ten years old again.

This is crazy, he thought to himself. He could not get over how great it felt to be a kid again.

After a long night of candy and mischief, Louis and his friends were getting tired. On their way back to Rodney's house, the three boys ran into a group of bullies from their neighborhood.

"Look who it is," the leader of the bullies said. There were four of them, and they were four years older than Louis and his friends.

"Leave us alone!" said Miles.

"Where's the candy?" said one of the bullies as they got closer to Louis and his friends.

Louis looked down at himself in first person view and remembered that he was just a small child. He was not sure if his grown man fighting skills would be useful in his younger body. Let alone if he was any stronger than he was back then.

He looked over at Rodney and Miles and took a deep breath. The bullies got closer as the boys backed up further and further. Louis closed his eyes and started to meditate like he had been doing as of late. He remembered his breathing exercises and cleared his mind as the bullies continued to intimidate them.

Then Louis opened his eyes and yelled, "Miles, Rodney. Run!"

The three boys darted in the other direction. The bullies followed suit. They chased after Louis and his friends until the three came to a dead end. As the older kids got closer, Louis opened Rodney's backpack and took out a carton of eggs.

As they got even closer, Louis cocked an egg back and launched it at them making it explode. Yolk splashed all over one of the bullies. Then Miles and Rodney grabbed more eggs and hurled them at the bullies. Louis had a moment of self-realization. Back then, they got beat up by the bullies, who also robbed their candy. The event had traumatized him, ruining Halloween for many years to come.

Louis refused to let this do-over opportunity go to waste.

He ran at the bullies and jumped in the air throwing both his legs up in front of him. Soaring through the air Louis finally connected with one of them. His shoe nearly went through the head bully's chest, dropping him to the ground before Louis fell on top of him on his way down.

On instinct, he began throwing punches in each direction at all four of them. This type of wildcard strategy scared the older kids half to death. They started to step back before they all turned around and ran away.

"Louis! That was amazing," said Miles.

"You're like... my hero," said Rodney.

Louis took the remaining three eggs and launched them at the last house before the dead end. "Run!" he yelled as the boys left the scene of the crime.

After reliving his childhood for a day, the lights began to dim, and the level was coming to an end. Cody said into the loudspeaker, "Great job, Louie. Now remember, we gotta go right into Day Two. You got a date picked out yet? We only have forty-five seconds to decide, or the game will decide for you."

Louis was unable to see. Everything was pitch black, but he could hear Cody. He could not decide. Time was running out.

"I don't know!" yelled Louis.

"I got it," said Jack. "Step aside." He walked over and put in the date of the night Louis cheated on his wife.

"What are you doing?" asked Cody as his boss took over.

Jack punched in the date: September 29, 2018. He knew every single one of Louis' memories, and he did whatever he wanted. Cody became frustrated as he watched his boss take over the system. Jack pushed "Enter" into the action center and the game began to load.

"This will be interesting," Jack said as he walked away and gave Cody his seat back.

"What's going on?" asked Louis.

"Nothing, Lou. Just got a great idea," said Jack.

"What happened to free will?" asked Cody as he watched the monitor.

"He couldn't pick a date. Better for me to choose than the game. Lord knows what it would have picked. He could have come out in his mother's god damned belly for all we know," said Jack. "Trust me, this will be great. Rip the bandage off. See what Version Two is really made of."

"Whatever you say, Jack, you're the boss," said Cody as he turned away and rolled his eyes.

JEFF YAGER

Seven Days VR finished loading and Louis was transported through the quantum realm where he would end up back on the single worst day of his life.

Louis respawned inside his car, reeking of booze, and driving down the rough side of town. He was scoping out different girls that worked on the street.

He was stuck in the same mindset as he was that night. Still slightly aware that he was in the game even though it felt terribly real. Which apparently it was. He saw the lady of the night that caught his eye the first time and pulled his car up. Louis rolled down his window. She turned around and bent over before saying, "Hey sugar! Want some company?"

Then he had an epiphany.

Something came over him and he replied, "Actually, no. I'm all right." He threw a hundred dollars in cash out of the window and drove away. Louis sped down the street and onto the main road to go home to his wife and kids.

"Anybody got some popcorn?" asked Jack. He watched the flat screen monitors as Louis showed character and changed his mind at the last moment. "Things just got good," he said. "Somebody make some damn popcorn already!" Jack sat in his chair and kicked his feet up on the desk as he watched his star employee relive one of the worst nights of his life.

Louis pulled up in his driveway before turning off his car and locking it. He was relieved and happy with himself for not ultimately going through with cheating on her. He wished it was the decision that he made in the first place. But he was grateful to have a second chance. Most people do not get second chances.

He unlocked the front door and made his way upstairs to his room. It was almost midnight. As he got closer to his bedroom, he heard a strange sound. It seemed like their bed was rocking back and forth and smacking against the wall. A heavy feeling of regret passed over him as he got closer. He listened with his ear against the door before kicking it open by breaking the lock. Denise was in bed with another man. A man that was younger, taller, and in much better shape than he was. Anger flowed through Louis' veins as he could not believe his eyes. He charged at the man in his bed and smashed his right fist into his jaw, knocking him off his own bed.

"I should kill you!" he screamed as he kicked the naked man in the ribs.

"Lou!" pleaded Denise.

Something came over him and Louis stopped when he remembered what happened the first time. It was ironic and also hypercritical for him to blame her. He looked at his wife, disappointed beyond belief.

Louis stormed down the stairs and out the front door. "Idiot!" he yelled as he jumped into his car and reversed it out of his driveway. "Stupid!" he said to himself as he looked in the rearview mirror. Then, after a minute of driving, he started to laugh out loud at the situation. "Who woulda thunk it?" He looked at himself in the rear-view mirror before he started to cry.

He drove to the highway and left the city. He got a room at a hotel until the VR day was done and he could go back to reality. He did not want to play the game anymore.

Jack watched the monitors before eating a handful of popcorn from his bowl. "Now this is what I mean. This game is going to change the world."

"Or at least his world," said Cody as he felt awful for Louis. He was really starting to like the guy. He did not agree with his boss and thought the worst was yet to come.

"This is epic. We're onto something here, boys. Great job, everyone. Job well done," said Jack.

"At least he's going to get a nice paycheck," Cody said grudgingly to Jack as he walked over to help Louis unplug from the *Seven Days VR*.

Chapter 16

The night sky lit up bright with a full moon that appeared much larger than usual. As he watched the moon, Louis reflected on his first two days of Version Two. He was not sure what to make of it all. At first, he was mad that Jack took it upon himself and picked his day for him. But he was relieved to find out what happened that day when he got his second chance.

He kept thinking maybe it was karma for what he did. He could not believe his wife was cheating, but he also could not blame her. It even gave him a small sense of relief that she was just as bad as him. He wondered what this could have changed. How catching her would have made a difference. But he was afraid to call her. It was all so bizarre. He did not know what to do. Louis wondered what could have changed in his real life now that the past was completely redone.

Outside of his new house, Louis watched as the clouds slowly floated in front of the moon making it disappear for nearly ten seconds before displaying itself again. He rubbed his beard as he thought, *what have I gotten myself into?*

Louis reached into his pocket and pulled out his pack of cigarettes. He looked at them and wondered where he went wrong and why he was still a slave to nicotine and tobacco. His body instinctively pulled one out as he sparked his yellow lighter and put the flame to the end of the cigarette. He inhaled until an orange ember grew thick just before letting out a cloud of smoke that gathered high up in the sky before breaking apart into the air.

Louis took another drag and looked at the cigarette. Then he realized what he would do with his third day in the game. He would go back to the day that he began smoking, and simply never smoke that first cigarette.

He figured if he never started smoking then he may have been able to prevent a lifetime of this unhealthy and disgusting habit.

It has to work, he thought to himself as he took one more puff of the Bearstick Menthol 100 before flicking it into the road.

For the next few days, Louis slept a lot as he recovered from the first beta testing days. But within a week, Louis felt well enough to go back to work at the Mindtrick building.

As he and Cody reviewed the results, they concluded that Days One and Two were successful, even if they might have been hard for Louis to relive.

"And I'm sorry for that bull-crap Jack pulled last time. I don't know why he did that," said Cody.

"Oh, it's okay. I figured it was Jack who picked the day. But honestly, it's all good. I'm not even mad."

Louis explained to him how things were not that different with Denise, though. Not much had changed apart from Louis getting to see his kids more frequently than before he started working for Mindtrick. This time, Denise felt a major amount of guilt for getting caught cheating. Louis felt less guilt but had some iffy feelings about how he got the weight off of his chest. Even though he never cheated in her eyes, he still remembered doing it himself. And that memory would not go away, regardless of the timeline of events. They were still divorced. Things just seemed more balanced to him. Although it is unlikely that it made any difference at all.

Jack walked in the room with a coffee in each hand. "Louie, my man, take this," he said as he handed him one of the cups.

"Jack, hey. Sorry about the other day. Forgot the part about picking two dates. Had a brain fart," said Louis as he took a sip from his cup of coffee. "But you came through in the clutch. You caught me off guard at first. However, I'm glad you did it."

"Don't even mention it, my friend, No worries, at all. But I must say, wow. That was some heavy shit, my guy," said Jack as he chugged his coffee before letting out a subtle burp. "That's damn good," he said as he put his mug down on the table in the virtual lab.

"Yeah, guess it was pretty...weird," said Louis. "But I feel better now, for some reason."

Cody watched Jack. He had tons of things to say, but kept his lips sealed in fear of losing his job if he spoke out. But he was angry, to say the least, as well as completely disgusted by his boss. He was worried about what would happen next, and that he had helped create something that could be used for evil. He already saw it unfolding. But he was concerned it was too late to stop Jack from doing whatever he was secretly planning. Cody was beginning to think Jack was a madman. Then he looked over at the team who were busy typing away, adding new code to the system that would enhance the game moving forward.

"We can't dwell on the past though, am I right?" said Jack before laughing and putting his hand up for a high five. He paused and waited until a team member gave him one. He continued, "Today is a new day. Let's make it a good one, shall we?"

"Indeed, it is," said Cody as he snapped out of his internal thought process.

For Day Three, Louis told Cody he'd decided to go back to the day he began smoking. He was at a party that his friend Tanner was throwing, and a girl from his French class, Amber, offered him a smoke.

This time he declined the girl's offer and instead left the party altogether. It seemed crazy to Louis that he did not have the urge to smoke. He had not felt that way in what seemed a lifetime. He remembered the act of smoking, but he did not crave it.

He spent the rest of his day hanging out with his friend, Miles, who he had remained close with over the years ever since he stood up to the bullies on Halloween. Before he played Seven Days VR and changed the past, they barely spoke to each other after middle school.

The two got some bacon cheeseburgers at BeefBoys and caught a movie the next day. They went to see "Blazing Bananas" starring Harvey Chandler. Louis could not believe he still had no desire to smoke.

As the day ended, Louis came back to reality. Only now, he was thirty-two pounds heavier than he was before Day Three. He remembered smoking in the back of his mind, but he had no feeling or temptation to do so. His plan worked.

He got out of his body suit and changed into his normal clothes. He grimaced when he noted the size he now wore, but decided it was worth it because he was breathing much better. He was taking much longer and bigger breaths. It was mindboggling. Then he stared at himself in the mirror and could not believe how much bigger he'd gotten. He figured that giving up smoking must have left him to cope with stress over the years in other ways, like eating. He was proud of himself for going back and making sure he never picked up the smoking habit. Then he felt kind of bad that the only way he could quit smoking was with the help of a videogame.

Better late than never, he thought to himself.

Chapter 17

The next morning, Louis could still not believe it worked. And all he had to sacrifice was adding a few pounds, which was worth not having to light up a cigarette every thirty minutes.

Holy shit. Would you look at that, said Louis, rubbing his large belly. *I think I could get used to this.*

Now that the past was altered, and he was not the one caught cheating, the courts awarded Louis more days with his children.

He took Natalie to the mall for a spontaneous shopping spree. He let her pick out anything she wanted. She had him get her all the outfits she always saw in the windows of her favorite store. Now her Dad could afford almost anything she wanted. And she did not hesitate to take advantage of it while it lasted.

All Louis bought at the mall was food from three different places in the food court. He would get full, digest, and be ready to go again. His appetite was endless.

His daughter was grossed out by her father stuffing his face constantly, but she was not complaining as she watched him scarf down a cheeseburger. She now had dozens of bags filled with designer clothes to wear to school. "Take it easy, Dad," she said as he finished up the last bits of his burger. "I don't want you to choke."

"I'm fine, Natty, don't worry about me," said Louis as he grabbed a handful of fries. "Want one?" he asked. She shook her head no, then looked at her new hat in admiration.

A week later, Louis walked into work and greeted Emily at the front desk, "Good morning, sunshine."

"Hello, Mr. Parker. Lovely weather we are having isn't it?" said Emily as a smile formed on her face.

"Why, yes, it is, Emily," said Louis.

"Looking sharp," she said.

"Thank you for noticing. You look quite nice yourself," he responded.

"Thank you, Louie. Good luck today," said Emily.

"I appreciate that, hon. Thanks!"

Louis walked to his office, greeting most employees as they passed by. He felt like he was appreciated at his job, and it was great.

Everyone in the building seemed to know him by name, but he had yet to learn all their names in return. Some of his co-workers would look at him with a welcoming reception like they knew things. Perhaps things about Louis that he may not even know himself. But his bank account prevented him from overthinking that sort of thing. He kept on trucking along until he reached his new office. He walked up to find a sign on the door that read, "Mr. Louis."

For Day Four, Louis chose one of the most disturbing days of his life. That was the day his much-loved older sister Kelly died in a horrific car crash. He knew it could be risky picking that day, but he figured it was worth a shot if he could somehow save her life and bring her back. Cody warned him prior to the level that the quantum reciprocator was acting up, so if he started to feel funny or out-of-whack for any reason, Louis needed to go to a safehouse in the game and wait there until the level is complete to avoid any major mishaps or malfunctions.

He got the idea to pick that day when his daughter had recently asked if he ever thought about his sister. It made Louis break down in tears as memories began to come back to him. He loved his sister and missed her every day of his life. He always said he would do anything to get her back, and this was his chance.

Louis spawned to when he was twenty-one years old, working at the BeefBoys burger joint. This time, after work, he would go to the party his sister had invited him to. Originally, he skipped it because he was too tired and had ended up going home.

Jack walked into the virtual room to watch the monitor with Cody and the team. As the day went on, they watched Louis play the game. He was driving to the party to join his sister.

"This should be fun," said Jack followed by a rather insidious laugh. The team laughed with him to avoid any awkwardness. Jack hated when people did not laugh with him. He made that very apparent. Everyone at Mindtrick knew that. Always laugh with Mr. Jack.

Louis arrived at the party. People were standing wall to wall, drinking, smoking, as well as doing other drugs that Louis was unable to identify from a distance. He did not feel comfortable at all and just wanted to find his sister as fast as he could. He wanted to get out of there. He did not recognize anyone except for one of his sister's friends. He could not remember his name, but he went up to him and asked, "Hey, have you seen my sister?"

"Yeah, she's upstairs with Blake, I think," the guy responded.

"Who the hell is Blake?" Louis asked. "Never mind, thanks."

Louis headed upstairs until he saw his sister running toward the stairs. "Leave me alone!" she yelled as a man followed her out of a bedroom.

"Kelly!" said Louis as she passed him on the stairs.

She turned around and said, "Louie?" and kept going. She went out the front door and headed toward her car. She appeared extremely intoxicated. Louis followed his sister outside.

"Wait up!" he yelled as he chased her.

The man she was yelling at ran out and said, "Kelly! Please, wait!"

"Back off!" said Louis. He shoved Blake to the ground. "Leave my sister alone."

"Screw you, Blake!" she yelled, fumbling for her car keys.

"Whatever," said Blake as he went back inside the house.

Louis grabbed Kelly's purse, looked inside, and found her keys. Then he turned around and chucked them into the woods as far as he could. The sky was turning purple.

"What the hell!" she said. "Why would you do that?" asked his sister as she punched him in the arm.

"You wouldn't understand. But I had to do that, Kelly," said Louis as he stopped her from punching him again. Then he hugged her and said, "I love you. I can't see you go again."

"What?" she asked, as she pushed her brother away.

"Nothing," he said as he looked in the woods to make sure he could not spot the keys. At least now he knew she would not be driving anytime soon.

The next day, Louis woke up from getting some much-needed rest after the last session of *Seven Days*. He felt a weight lifted off his shoulders, thinking that he had done something good. He thought if all went according to plan, his sister was alive and well. Kelly was somewhere out there living her best life. He got ready for the day and did a little bit of meditation.

A slight feeling of darkness passed over him. Like there was something wrong. Like he had made a terrible mistake. He had no clue what, or why, but something did not feel right. He took a deep breath in as the guided meditation video played from his cell phone. He sat with his feet crossed and his hands to his sides. He inhaled again slowly, before exhaling even slower.

After he picked up a twenty-piece order of chicken nuggets at the drive-through of Bokbusters, he drove to work.

Louis was not sure what was going on anymore, but so far, the trial was going well in his opinion. He thought he was doing the best he could testing the new game.

He sat in his car in the Mindtrick parking lot. He could not get past the feeling that something was off. He decided to pull out his phone to text his brother, Roy.

"I know this is random as all hell…but… have you talked to Kelly recently?" he wrote before hitting the send button.

He ate a few nuggets. Then he got a text back. Roy replied, "This is a joke, right?"

"No, what? Have you?" Louis wrote.

Minutes passed. Then another text came in. This one read, "You know damn well I haven't talked to that monster in years, Lou."

Louis did not know what to make of the text. He finished up his nuggets, turned off his car, got out, and locked it.

Louis made his way inside the Mindtrick lobby. He waved to Emily at the front desk. As he walked by, she stared deep into his eyes. It almost felt like she was trying to read his soul. It gave Louis the creeps as he made his way down the long hallway toward the lab.

Louis got to the lab where Jack was having a meeting with the team. He noticed that Cody was not there. He just assumed he must have taken the day off or something. But in the back of his mind, he knew there was something wrong. Something was up, and he could feel it. He just did not know what. He was anxious to find out what happened to his sister, and if his plan had worked. He wondered where in the world she was. All he wanted to do was see her for the first time in over twenty years. But the text from Connor left Louis to worry.

"Where's Cody?" Louis asked.

Jack paused what he was saying to the team and looked over at Louis.

"Hey Louie, take a seat...sit down."

Louis sat at the table surrounded by the team of coders. They looked over at him and smiled, then turned back to their boss.

"Listen, we had to let Cody go. I don't want to get into all the details right now. But his time with us has unfortunately come to an end. He will be missed," said Jack.

"Well…that…sucks," said Louis as he wondered what could have happened. He had gotten close to Cody during his time there. He could not imagine what he could have done to get fired just like that, out of nowhere. Cody seemed like Jack's go-to guy.

"I could really use a coffee right now. Anybody else?" said Jack. "Louie? How about a coffee?"

"I'm good," Louis responded.

Chapter 18

On his way home from work, Louis got a call from Cody and immediately picked it up. "Hey!" he said as he made a right turn on Destiny Road. He stuck his hand into the bag of cheezepuffs that had become intrinsic to his day. He needed to snack all day. He gained nearly fifty-seven pounds since he began playing Seven Days VR.

"I'm sure you heard the news by now. Jack canned my ass," said Cody.

"Yeah. I was worried. What the hell happened?" asked Louis.

"Kinda too much to explain over the phone," said Cody. "Let's just say, I overstepped my bounds and called the prick out during the last trial day. One thing led to another, and security escorted me out of the building. Seven years I've been at that company. Seven god damned years."

"Geesh, man, that's rough," said Louis.

"Sure is. But don't worry about it. I'll be fine."

"I know you will," said Louis.

"But hey, listen. There's something you should know. About your sister. I'm sending you a link. Stay calm…but it's not great. Something happened during your last level. Things took a weird turn and…well…I'll let you see for yourself. But don't freak out. Everything will be okay," said Cody.

"Umm, okay," said Louis nervously. "What's going on, Cody?"

"Just read the news article I send you. You'll learn everything you need to know."

"All right."

"Gotta go, keep in touch. You're one of the good ones, Louie," said Cody before he ended the call.

Louis kept driving. A couple minutes later he got a text from Cody containing a link from an old news article that dated back to December 2010. Then he looked up and saw he was about to collide with a car in front of him. Louis swerved out of the way at the last second. He decided he would read the article when he got home because he knew it was unsafe and maybe even illegal to text and drive.

Louis finally made it home. He parked his car in the garage and went inside.

Louis took a seat on his couch and pulled out his phone. He opened the article that Cody had sent him. At first, he refused to believe it.

The headline read, "Woman Stabs Boyfriend in Heated Rage."

What the hell? His vision became blurry, so he rubbed his eyes and began to read.

Police last night arrested Kelly Parker, 34, for the murder of her boyfriend, Paul Ramirez, 36. Ramirez was pronounced dead at the scene.

Sources say that Parker stabbed Ramirez once in the stomach. Parker called 911 herself.

Once local officers arrived on the scene, they put Parker in handcuffs and arrested her on suspicion of first-degree murder of Paul Ramirez. Sources say she did not resist arrest. She also confessed at the scene.

Neighbors reported hearing loud banging from the couple's apartment earlier in the night. Her friend Bella

Caprina, who lived across the hall, said that Kelly was a "soft spoken, sweet, gentle soul who would not harm a fly."

Another neighbor said they saw the couple fighting multiple times for months in the hallway or in the elevator leading up to the murder.

If found guilty, Parker could face the maximum penalty, life without parole.

We will watch this story closely as new information comes in.

Louis was deeply disturbed by what he read. He threw his phone across his living room and began to cry.

Over the next couple of hours, he went from feelings of sadness and depression to stress and anger. He could not fathom his beloved and gentle big sister doing anything like that. He looked up more articles about the incident to learn as much as he could. He found out that she was ultimately sentenced to twenty-five years to life in prison.

He also found an article that included an interview with her from years later where Kelly explained that she acted in self-defense. After years of physical abuse from her boyfriend, she finally stood up for herself. It went much further than she ever expected it to and ended with her taking his life. She also said when she stabbed him, she must have blacked out, which is why she thinks she kept attacking him and did not stop until she awoke from the trance that she was in. But it was too late to save her boyfriend.

Louis felt a cloud of regret come over him, wondering if he had done the wrong thing by preventing her death in the car accident. He tried to imagine what her life had been like, and if spending twenty-five years behind bars was better or worse than her original fate. He thought he was doing something good by stopping her death. Louis had assumed she would marry and have a family and live a happy life. He never considered anything bad might happen to her, especially anything as horrific as the physical abuse she endured followed by her conviction and imprisonment for first degree murder. He had no clue of the chain reaction of events that he might set into motion simply by trying to do the right thing. Then Louis wondered what other butterfly effect changes could have occurred since he had started working at Mindtrick.

Maybe I should have left after Version One, he thought.

The next day, Louis was still torn up over the whole situation with his sister and did not know what to think anymore. He sat on his couch with his laptop on his footstool. He was reading more articles about his sister. He was absolutely horrified by what she had done. He blamed himself for picking such a traumatic day to relive because now he could not undo what he had changed. He also thought maybe he could have done something to stop her from taking her boyfriend's life that night.

Then he had an idea. Maybe that could be the next day he chose to relive?

"I've got three days left," Louis said to himself before he cracked open a cold beer.

"Huh?" asked Tommy who was on the other couch.

"Oh, sorry, nothing."

"So, how's work been?" asked Tommy.

"Well. I mean…you know, it's been kind of stressful lately," said Louis as he shut his laptop and put it on the charger.

"Oh man. Is your mind starting to play tricks on you already?" said his son before laughing. "Get it? Because you work at Mindtrick?"

"Hah, yeah, good one. Maybe leave the Dad-jokes to your old man," said Louis. "Hey Tommy, can I ask you something?"

"Sure, what's up?"

"Well, this is random I know, but…do you remember your Aunt Kelly?" he asked.

"What? Of course, I remember Aunt Kelly. How could I forget her? She was my favorite relative until… until, well, you know. Matter of fact, she's still one of my favorites now that I think about it."

"Yeah," said his father as he took a swig of beer.

Louis texted Cody and asked him if he would come over so they could talk.

After dinner with his kids, Louis heard a knock on the door. It was Cody. He opened it up and gave him a big hug.

Cody patted him on the back and said, "I'm so sorry, Louie. Never expected anything like that to happen."

Inside the house, the two were having a beer on the couch. Louis finally mentioned the big black eye on Cody's face as well as the bandage on his cheek.

"So, what happened to you?" asked Louis.

"What do you think? Jack. Jack is what happened to me," Cody said as he took a drink.

"No way," Louis said. "What the hell happened?"

"Let's turn off our phones and put them somewhere else. You never know if that asshole is listening in or not. I wouldn't even be surprised if the shitbag has your house bugged by now, to be honest," Cody said.

"Really?"

"Yeah, actually…we should take a step outside. Let's get some fresh air," said Cody.

"Sure," said Louis as he got up off the couch.

The two left their phones on the couch and went out back. They took their beers with them. Louis and Cody stood in the backyard, where Cody felt safer and more willing to discuss what was going on.

"So, fill me in, man," said Louis.

"All right. Long story short...Jack took it into his own hands to mess with the results from Day Four of your trial. Once you stopped your sister from driving that night, he took control of the system. He pushed me out of the way and entered in a series of code called the 'Doomsday Device'. This gives Jack the power to alter the outcome of the game, and ultimately...well...your life. Once he did that, he added a little bit of extra chaos code. He didn't necessarily plan for that exact chain reaction, but he did make sure it would be totally traumatizing...whatever happened. He wanted to see what would happen if he pushed the game to its absolute limit. And he used you as his lab rat." Cody took another sip of his beer.

"I'm trying to understand. It doesn't make any sense. But I trust you, man, I believe you," said Louis.

"Good, you should. So anyway, once I saw what he was doing...I couldn't take it anymore and watch him screw up your life more than he already has. I got up and pulled him out of his seat and away from the keyboard. But the damage was done. He managed to apply the Doomsday Device and there was nothing I could do to stop him. I tried everything I could, but it was too late."

Louis stared at Cody in shock as he continued to explain what happened. He stroked his beard in disbelief.

"Then I turned around and Jack bashed me in the face with a steel clipboard. I tried to put up a fight and defend myself, but the team bombarded me and restrained me. Then, Jack sucker punched me a few times as the team had me trapped with nowhere to go. Security guards showed up and escorted me out of the building. On my way out, I could hear Jack yelling, 'You're fired, Cody. Good luck finding a job in this town, blah blah blah.' Or at least words to that effect. I'm not too sure. It's all a bit fuzzy now that I think back to it. But yeah, that's why I was fired. And that's why I have this nice bruise and cut as a souvenir."

"Damn...I don't know what to say," said Louis.

"You don't have to say anything," said Cody. "It's my own fault for trying to get in his way. I should have known it wouldn't work. But I was so pissed watching what he was doing to you, I couldn't help it. The man is evil incarnate."

Louis could not believe what he was hearing. Cody continued, "Look, I've come to find out some disturbing news about what Jack has planned when this game drops. If you think the social media CEOs were bad for trying to control and monetize our data and personal information, just wait until you see what Jack has in store. The man wants to have complete and utter control of our memories, our dreams, our subconscious as well as our own self-consciousness as a whole. This goes much further than videogames, Louie. Jack has some sinister shit coming our way. Oh, and by the way...I found out what Jack was putting in the coffee. All of our coffee. It is a drug called Portomazine. It keeps people docile and highly susceptible to mind control. Mr. Jack has been poisoning our brains this whole time."

Louis finished his beer and said, "Screw this. I'm done. There's no way I'm going back to work for that sociopathic psycho." He could not believe what he was hearing from Cody. Now the coffee thing really started to make more sense to him.

"No. Louie. As much as I want you to quit, you can't. If you do, Jack will...how do I put this...well, Jack will kill you. Or better yet, have you killed. I'm almost certain. And if he doesn't kill you, he will find some way to make your life a living hell. And if he can't get to you, he will find your children, your ex-wife, everyone you know and love. And he will make sure they disappear in the night. Vanish in the wind. It's even in the contract, which I'm sure you didn't read entirely. Don't worry. No one does. But yeah, Jack practically owns you as long as you're still testing the game."

Louis looked at Cody and sighed, "Well, shit. What am I going to do? What can I do?"

"I'm still trying to figure that part out. Trust me— if I had a plan already, I would have mentioned it. I'm sorry you had to get caught up in all of this, Louie."

"Dang, well. I'm shit out of luck, then. I can't live with the idea that because of me, my sister Kelly killed her abusive boyfriend and now she's been sitting in prison for all these years. You're saying there's no way we can undo the changes that happened because I changed the outcome on the day that Kelly would have died in that car accident?"

"Not necessarily," said Cody.

"How so?"

"Well, you still have three days left of the trial before you're done. If you try to quit now, then Jack will know we're onto him. But if you go back to work and act like nothing is wrong...you may just get out of this alive.

"You have one week left at Mindtrick, and that may give me enough time to come up with something. But you must keep going. That part, I know. I'm lucky the dude hasn't had me killed yet. But you're his golden ticket for the moment, and if he lost you, I'm sure he would react way worse than he did with me," Cody said.

"This is nuts, man. Not sure if I can even take anymore. Lord knows what the next levels will bring. I'll probably wake up to both my parents floating in a river somewhere. Or my brothers recruited by a terrorist organization or some shit."

"You're in too deep now. You gotta stay strong and ride this out until the end. You're a good guy, Louie. I know you don't deserve any of this," said Cody.

Louis looked at his house and said, "None of this is even worth it. The money, the house, none of it. I'm losing my mind, Cody. I learned to like the idea of getting second chances. Then it hit me, that things happen a certain way and even if there does not seem to be a reason, and even if the outcome might be regrettable, if you try to mess with the past, it messes everything up, apparently," said Louis, as he stroked his beard.

"Can't even imagine what you've been going through. Well, I've been watching but I haven't experienced it firsthand. I feel for you," said Cody.

"I'm done living in the past!" Louis exclaimed.

"I understand, Bro. I get it. Look, I gotta get going, but we will keep in touch. If anything goes wrong, or you need any advice, you can give me a shout and I'll try my best to help. Remember, be safe in the game and don't forget, if you die in the game…you die in real life. I can't stress that enough, Louie. Whatever you do, whatever day you go back to. Just protect yourself at all costs. No matter what Jack wants you to do," said Cody as he shook his hand and said, "Goodbye, Louie. Be strong."

Cody got his phone from the couch, then walked around the side of the house to his shiny blue car and drove off. A motorcycle was in the neighborhood and the sound irritated Louis before he went back inside.

Tommy was waiting by the back door. He caught a few moments of their conversation but had no clue what any of it meant. All he knew was his father was afraid, like he was in danger or something. He never saw his Dad afraid, and Tommy started to worry.

That night, Louis drowned himself in a pool of liquor. His mind was telling him to go get a pack of smokes, but his body did not crave it. He nearly finished a giant bottle of whiskey by himself. He was going back and forth between crying and moping. He thought about what Cody had told him, but he was not certain what he was going to do about it.

Louis came up with a few ideas for what he would select for his Day Five level. He was concerned that if he did not have a specific date in mind, Jack would decide it for him. That was the last thing he wanted to happen, now that he knew what Jack was capable of while he was stuck in virtual reality.

Louis jotted down dozens of days from his past, creating a web in his notebook of the best ones to consider next.

Louis got up to use the bathroom. On his way through the hallway of the second floor of his house, he saw a framed picture he had saved. The picture showed Louis with Denise and the kids when they were little. He thought back to the good times in their marriage when the kids were young. Many memories came to mind and Louis began to smile for the first time in what seemed like days.

A light bulb went off in his head and he had an idea. A crazy idea. But an idea to say the least.

The next morning, Louis dropped Tommy back off at Denise's place. When he pulled up and his son got out, Louis said, "I love you, Tommy. No matter what, I want you to know I love you. You are the greatest thing that ever happened to me. You and your sister. Tell her I love her too, please."

"No problem, old man," said Tommy as he walked to the front door. Denise opened the door to let him in. She waved at Louis. He tried to wave back, but tears took shape and fell from his watery eyes. He rolled up his window and sped off. His heart was pounding, and it was nearly impossible for him to relax. He tried to practice some of his meditation and breathing techniques as he drove down the road, but nothing seemed to work. His heart pumped and raced faster than usual. He was having a panic attack.

Around noon, Louis changed into his jumpsuit and awaited instructions to begin Day Five. The team was setting everything up.

Louis missed Cody, as he did not really trust anyone else at Mindtrick. To him, they all seemed like artificial intelligence drones that Jack had created in a lab—soldiers ready to do his bidding at any given moment.

This time, the lights in the virtual room appeared to have a red tint to them. That was new. He tried not to focus on that or get too carried away. It probably meant nothing. Louis took a deep breath as he looked up at the clock on the wall. Time was moving slowly. He just wanted to get it over with.

Once Louis was strapped in and ready to go, one of the coders that he had not recognized started up the game.

He looked at Louis and said, "Where are we going today, Louie?"

"Take me to the night that I met my ex-wife," he said as he took another deep breath before exhaling slowly.

"You got it," said the coder.

"By the way, I'm sorry but I don't think I caught your name."

"Cody," he said.

"Uhh…what?" asked Louis as he stretched his arms and legs in his VR bodysuit.

"Yeah, well…that's my name, don't wear it out," said the new Cody.

"Well, that's weird," said Louis.

I don't like this at all, he thought to himself.

"Sorry if you think I'm weird, sir," the coder said as he punched in the date Louis had requested.

"Is that your actual name?"

"Well, no. It's not. But Mr. Jack said that's my new nickname. And you don't want to argue with the boss, you know?" said the coder.

"Sure don't," Louis replied.

Before he could take another breath and try to relax, the game had already begun, and Louis was drifting off to the world of virtual reality. He had been transported through the quantum realm tunnel as his body morphed through time and space. The blackness turned to white as he flew through the portal. Once it loaded, Louis spawned in the game on the night that he and his brother, Connor, had gone to the local carnival with their current girlfriends. Connor was two years older than Louis. They were not as close as Louis was with Roy growing up.

Jack watched through the window as Louis commenced the next level of *Seven Days VR*. "Good boy," he said as he drank his coffee and walked away.

Meanwhile, at the carnival, Louis walked around as he did the first time around. Connor was doing everything he could to impress his date, while Louis barely paid attention to his. He kept getting these overwhelming senses of *Deja vu* as they wandered around the fair.

They went on a couple of rides. The Ferris wheel felt like it lasted even longer than it did originally. He had nothing in common with his date and could barely hold a conversation with her. He noticed he did not even try.

The night went on and the moment finally came where Louis would meet Denise. She was working at one of the food booths. Connor's girlfriend, Paula, wanted to eat, so they took a break from walking around to grab some nachos and a few candy apples.

Louis and Denise locked eyes the way they had the original night they met. She was just as beautiful as he remembered. He tried to play it cool, like he did the first time around.

"Can I help you?" asked Denise as she handed another customer a cup of soda and put some cash in the register.

Louis was at a loss for words, as so many happy memories from their marriage played back in his head. He could not believe he messed it all up with such an amazing woman that he once adored. She was perfect in his eyes. He began to have a lot of realizations once he was reminded how beautiful she was when they first met. She was sweeter than the candy apples hanging above the counter.

"Hello? Anybody in there?" said Denise as Louis drifted off admiring her gorgeous eyes and fit figure.

"I'm sorry for my dweeb of a brother," said Connor. "Can we get two orders of nachos with extra cheese? Oh, and four candy apples, please," Connor continued as he took his place in line and covered for Louis who looked completely lost and out of place.

"Sure thing," Denise said, as she prepared their order.

"Real smooth," Connor said to Louis. "But I totally understand. The girl is a smoke show."

Louis, Connor, and their dates sat at a nearby bench and ate. When they were done, Connor got up and went to the counter. Denise handed him some napkins. Then Louis looked over and saw Connor reach over the counter and slip a piece of paper to her before whispering something in her ear. She laughed in a flirtatious way and then helped another customer as his brother walked away.

Connor got back to the table and whispered to Louis, "I doubt she'll call, but I gave the candy apple girl my number. You never know, right?"

Louis did not think too much of it because he knew he'd be back the following day to confess that he liked her, which ultimately led to their first date. He doubted anything would change, even though he was starting to feel a tiny bit concerned.

The next day, Louis got ready to return to the carnival to talk to Denise, just as he had the first time. The game had helped him rekindle that strong positive connection that propelled them into a courtship and then a marriage. He was starting to feel nostalgic about how much in love they used to be, and about the good times he and his wife had had before they let the daily frustrations of money and chores become more important than their feelings for each other.

What he failed to consider was the fact that his day in VR would end hours before he would get to see or talk to her again. He had not planned out the timing in this level as much as he would have if Cody was still there.

The game shut off and Louis lifted his VR headset. "Shit!" Louis yelled. Every person in the room snapped to attention. "Shit. What have I done?" Louis ripped off all of his equipment and ran out of the room before they could analyze him like they normally would.

On his way out of the building, he ran past Jack who tried to stop him by saying, "Louie! How you feeling?"

"Not now, Jack!" he responded as he darted through the halls and out of the building. He was still in his jumpsuit before he remembered he had to go back to the locker room to change and grab his car keys, wallet, and phone.

Once in his car, he started to panic. Louis had no clue what to expect…but he had a feeling that things might have gone horribly wrong. *SHIT, SHIT, SHIT*, he yelled to himself.

He looked at his phone. Nine missed calls and over twenty text messages. Most of them were from Cody. Then he saw one that stood out. A text was from his brother, Connor.

The message read, "Hey loser. Denise wants to know if you're coming to our barbeque next week."

Louis stopped short in the middle of the road, as he felt his heart skip a beat for a moment. He reread the message over and over and said to himself, "No way. What does that even mean, Connor?"

Once home, Louis pulled out his laptop and opened his brother's social media profile. He could not breathe for a second. Then he tried practicing his meditation techniques before he gave up. He looked at his brother's profile and find some troubling information. Under relationship status it read married....to Denise Parker. He opened his pictures folder to find photos of his brother Connor and Denise, as well as their two kids. He looked closer. The children had an eerie resemblance to Tommy and Natalie, but they were completely different, nonetheless. The caption for one of the pictures read, "Terry and Nina at the beach".

Louis began to cry.

What have I done?

Chapter 19

It was sunset. The orange sky slowly turned pink before fading to black. The first stars made their appearance. The moon stood out in the night sky as it lit up the stars that surrounded it.

Louis sat on a park bench and watched a group of runners go by. He was not sure what to make of everything. He was scared. He went into his phone and tried to dial his son again. An automated recording kept coming on saying that it was not a working number. He was confused and did not know what to do.

What's going on? he thought to himself.

A family of four ducks swam in the pond in front of him. It looked like a mom, dad, and two baby ducks. He could not help but be reminded of his own family before he and Denise had gotten divorced. Certain memories were harder to pinpoint than others as they were slowly fading away.

Louis felt that his entire life was now a lie. Like his past was not real to anyone except for him.

And beneath it all, he also felt a growing hatred for Jack. He was angry at himself for letting someone play around with his life like this. But he had no idea what he could do about it.

If he called Connor and told him what happened, he knew there was no way that Connor would ever believe him. He could not even believe it himself.

He thought he was going crazy as he cuddled up to his bottle of whiskey and the beer to wash it down. He felt defeated. All hope was gone.

Later on, Louis paced back and forth in his living room. He had a throbbing headache he could not get rid of. He figured alcohol was the best medicine at the time. Maybe he would move onto something more powerful later. He was helpless.

Louis picked up his phone and finally texted his brother: "Sorry Connor. Don't think I'll be able to make the BBQ. I got something planned already."

He got up to find the picture of him and his family. When he picked it up, there was no one in the photo except himself. For a few hopeful seconds he thought he might be hallucinating, so he splashed cold water on his face to see if he was dreaming or something. He was not. It was as if his entire marriage was all a figment of his own imagination.

Louis called a cab to take him to a nearby bar. He did not feel like drinking alone anymore. He wanted to surround himself with other intoxicated people so he wouldn't feel so bad. This did not work as his anxiety grew stronger after only an hour at the bar.

He stumbled out the door and joined the group of smokers out front. For a moment, he considered asking one of them for a cigarette, but instead blurted out, "How do you people even smoke those things? Disgusting!" he yelled before walking away and down the street.

One guy responded by yelling back, "Screw you, jackass! This is America! Where freedom lives!"

Louis then turned around and responded by saying, "It is what it is. Wait until you see what the future has in store for you. Then we'll see who's free."

Cars drove past as Louis tried to remember his old life, the one before he started *Seven Days VR*. He was tempted to throw himself into traffic and end it all. Why keep living? The idea of death sounded better and better the more he contemplated it. He tried to remember why he ever took the job at Mindtrick to begin with. The money was a major factor, but something else deep down inside of him had been excited about getting to relive his past. Only for it to come back and haunt him. He wished he'd never taken this trip down the rabbit hole. He wished he'd kept things the way they were. Things were just fine, when he thought back.

There's a reason everyone says, "be careful what you wish for," Louis thought to himself as he downed another swig of whiskey.

His phone was at 10% battery when it started ringing. He saw it was Cody, who had been leaving messages for a while now. Louis answered, slurring his words. "Cody-number-one! How's life? Because mine's pointless. But I'm sure you already knew that!"

"Louie, I've been trying to get ahold of you. I heard what happened. I'm terribly sorry, dude. One of the coders updated me and I can't believe what Jack pulled this time. I can't even imagine how you feel right now."

"I feel...well...I feel drunk!" said Louis as he tripped over a bag of trash on the sidewalk. "Dammit!" he yelled as he regained his balance and continued to stumble down the street.

"Look, did you read my texts?" asked Cody.

"Shit, no, sorry. Been a bit busy as of late. I can't do anything right these days," Louis replied as he slurred some more words.

"Well don't worry about it, I'll just tell you."

"I'm all ears!" said Louis as he took a seat on the curb to take a break from walking. His vision was blurred as he listened closer to Cody. The ringing in his other ear grew louder so he put his finger in it to hear Cody better.

"Okay. I may have a plan. Still putting it all together, but you might have a shot at getting your old life back, Louie. For real," said Cody.

"Don't mess with me, Bro," Louis slurred.

"Here's what you gotta do. The next day of testing, I want you to pick a day that…how do I put this…would excite Jack. Keep him intrigued, so he's in the virtual room long enough for me to hack into his computer and retrieve some private files. Files that could put him away for a long time. But you must keep him preoccupied. I'll need at least thirty minutes to access the data," Cody explained. "Does that make sense?"

"No…not really, but I'm in. You're the only one who looked out for me this whole time. I trust you," Louis said right before turning and puking. Some of it got on his shoes.

"You sound awful," said Cody.

"I know!" yelled Louis. He vomited again and said, "I'm sorry. I don't mean to yell at you, dude."

"It's all good," said Cody.

"I don't know, man. I hope this works. I pray that this works. And I rarely ever pray, you know," said Louis.

"I'll text this to you again in the event that you forget all of this by tomorrow. I'll use an app called Call Block that's untraceable so Jack can't see what we're saying to each other. Just in case he's trying to listen in on our conversations and shit," said Cody.

"You're a great friend, you know that?" said Louis.

"Just looking out. We'll talk soon, big Lou."

The next morning, Louis was hung over. He finally made his way to the kitchen where he chugged a gallon of water from the fridge until there was barely any left. He went into the bathroom and looked at himself in the mirror. *What have I become?* he said to himself before he started to brush his teeth. Slowly but surely, the taste of whiskey and vomit was diluted with toothpaste and mouthwash. Then Louis stepped into the shower. He turned the water to cold, hoping it would help him get out of the funk he was in. He was miserable beyond belief. He thought the pounding in his head from the hangover would last forever.

By the time Louis got to the office, he was rejuvenated. He'd reread all of Cody's messages that explained what he had to do. He was as ready as he would ever be. It was now or never. Day Six of the trials was on the way.

In the lobby, Emily greeted Louis with a big smile and said, "Good morning, Mr. Parker. Hope you have a great day."

Emily seemed older than most of the other administrative assistants at Mindtrick. Louis figured she was in her late thirties or even her early forties. He found himself looking at her left hand to see if she was wearing a wedding band, but he did not see one there. Working the desk, and putting in some time as Jack's secretary, Louis was told, were the entry level jobs for anyone who wanted to do coding or marketing for Mindtrick. Jack believed everyone who worked for his company had to master every job, from the ground up, even if that might mean washing the floors or making cold calls to potential gamers.

Emily glanced at Louis with eyes that followed him like a painting until he finally turned and walked away.

"Thanks!" he said before he headed to Jack's office.

He looked at the sign on the door that read "Mr. Jack". Goosebumps trickled down his spine as a dark vibe hovered over him. Louis knocked on the door, pushing it open. Jack turned his computer screen away quickly and said, "My guy! What's cracking, pal?" It appeared that Jack was doing something that he did not want anyone to see him doing. He always seemed to be hiding something.

"Hey, not much. Listen, I was wondering if you could oversee things today. You know, since I only have a couple days left working on the game. Would be nice to get some hands-on feedback from the genius behind it all, ya know?" said Louis.

Jack looked at him for a moment before a grin grew on his face. "Sure, Lou, why the hell not? I got nothing better to do at the moment. Let's see what you got for us today, buddy."

"Awesome," he responded. "You need a coffee or anything?" Louis asked.

"No, I'm good," said Jack. "Thanks for asking though. You know you don't have to do that sort of stuff,

Louie. I got lower people on the totem pole for that sorta thing. You are my main man, Lou. Don't forget it."

"Of course, Mr. Jack," said Louis.

Jack laughed and said, "C'mon, you know it's just 'Jack' to you. My main man! You can call me whatever the hell you please if you keep bringing me results like this, Lou."

In the virtual room, the team readied the game for Day Six of the trial run for the Version Two beta of *Seven Days VR*. Jack joined them with a full cup of Columbian brewed coffee and a bowl of popcorn to go with it. He made sure his new assistant, Jennifer, added extra butter.

Louis went to the locker room to grab his phone. He made sure the coast was clear before he texted Cody: "The eagle has landed. It's showtime."

"Noted," Cody replied promptly. Louis put his phone back in the locker and walked to the virtual room where the coders and Mr. Jack were waiting for him to get started. There was a lot riding on today's level, and Louis felt nervous.

Louis wanted to change everything back to the way it was, but he was not sure that was entirely possible. Cody made it seem like it was, but at this point, Louis was running low on hope. All of the money in the world could not fill the hole in his heart where his kids used to be.

He hoped that Jack would go to prison for all the wrongs he had done. Cody had told Louis about Jack's plans to monetize people's own memories and sell them off to the highest bidders online. The sky was the limit for what Jack was capable of, and Louis was starting to figure that out. Maybe it was time someone put a stop to the evil CEO once and for all. Louis was ready for whatever Cody wanted them to do.

"What day are we going with today, Louie?" asked the new Cody as he started up the game and console.

"Well..." said Louis. "I decided it's time to kick things into overdrive and do some real damage. I mean, my old life barely even exists at this point. Might as well take things to the next level, no pun intended. Or fuck it, pun intended. Let's turn up!"

"Now that's what I like to hear," said Jack as he took a bite of some popcorn. "Besides, my friend, you hated your old life...in my opinion this version of you is much, much better."

"Totally agree," said Louis as he nodded to Jack. "You did me a favor, Mr. Jack. I am forever grateful."

"Don't mention it," his boss replied. "I'm excited for what you have in store for us today! You know, Louie, they say we're living in a simulation. And you can tell everyone that it is true. However, you do have some free will, and therefore it is more of an augmented reality. So sure, we are living in a simulation metaphorically. For now, that is. Soon, we sure will be living in endless simulation loops, and we won't be able to decipher what's real and what's not. So anyway, Louie, where we going today, pal?"

"Well, I thought long and hard about it and I decided I'm going back to the day I skipped an audition for a small role in a movie. I always wanted to be an actor growing up. Might as well see what would have happened if I stuck to it," said Louis as he glanced at the clock. He prayed that Cody would have enough time to do what he needed to while Jack was busy in the virtual room with Louis and the crew of coders.

"Very, very interesting," said Jack. "I like it! Look at you, Louie, showing us some spunk! Some pizazz if you will! I'm really digging this side of you Louie, I can't lie."

"All right, we're all set. Got the date plugged in and ready whenever you are," said the new Cody.

The team got Louis prepared for the game and he gave the thumbs up. He took a deep breath in and exhaled as the game started to load.

Louis transported through the virtual realm as Level Six loaded. Sometimes teleporting felt like a minute, sometimes it felt like twenty. Louis had no real way of knowing how long the portal took in real life. This time, the teleportation through the past seemed to last several minutes before Day Six was set in motion. The game device and console were connected to the recently updated sensory regulator that would make for the most precise and exact algorithmic calculations.

He reemerged in Los Angeles, California to when he was twenty years old. He walked straight toward the building where casting auditions were being held. As he drew close, he felt the same doubts he'd had the first time he lived it. But now he kept moving and did not stop for anything.

When Louis arrived at the audition, he walked in and went up the stairs to the second floor where the producers and casting directors were set up. He signed in before taking a seat in the waiting room. There were at least ten other men there, waiting to audition as well. Louis tried to meditate for a moment when he realized he'd forgotten all the lines that he was supposed to remember. He asked one of the fellow actors what the lines were, but he was ignored. Everyone was too focused on landing the part themselves.

I'm screwed, he thought to himself.

After an hour and a half of waiting, Louis finally heard his name called, so he stood up and went inside the small room with a sign on it that read, "Auditions". He shook hands and greeted everyone in the room before he stepped in front of the green screen with a small video camera facing the front.

"Whenever you're ready," said one of the producers.

Meanwhile, back in real life...Cody was hacking into Jack's computer.

What he found was worse than he expected. Cody downloaded all the files he needed to incriminate his former boss. Cody had pinpointed crucial evidence of money laundering, embezzlement, fraud, memory/consciousness trading, past order receipts for Portomazine purchased on the company card, and even ties to human trafficking. He finished downloading the encrypted files with just a few minutes to spare.

Just like before, Jack added the Doomsday Device code into the game to alter all chain reactions and side effects from every action Louis took. Jack wanted to push the game to its limits.

Back in virtual reality, Louis got nervous for a moment as he could not remember the audition lines. He made a last-minute call to improvise. He began to recite a monologue he had remembered from one of his favorite actors, Leon Martino. The monologue was from the classic film, "Pushing Up Daisies". Louis started by quoting one of the most famous lines of the movie. "Maybe it's you, maybe it's me. But one thing is for certain, we're gonna get out of here alone, Marybeth. You hear me? We're gonna survive today, and sugar, I'm gonna make one hell of a wife out of you. Now don't you die on me, dammit!"

The producers were confused at first, but then became increasingly impressed by the fortitude Louis had shown by taking control and seizing the moment with a pungent poise and depth of character. It was original, and they had not seen anyone audition with passion like him all week. The monologue lasted a minute. When it was over, there was a brief silence in the room before one of the producers said, "Amazing!" The others began to clap. One of them even said, "Bravo. Bravo!"

Louis could not believe it worked. After he was done, he rejoined the others in the waiting room. Then the producers told everyone who'd auditioned to come back at five to get the results.

When Louis returned, he was delighted to hear he'd landed the role. It was a small role, but it had a few lines, more than most extras or background actors get in their entire career. Just enough that could lead him to bigger and better roles in the future.

"I truly appreciate the opportunity," said Louis. "I won't let you down."

"We know you won't," said one of the producers.

"We all think you're going to be a superstar," said another producer. "You got the 'it' factor."

"Wow, no one has ever told me that before," Louis responded.

"Glad I can be the first. Get used to it, sir," the head producer said.

The game finally ended after Louis spent the rest of the level watching movies at a local cinema that was near the location of the audition. He picked "Blueprint Blues" starring one of his heroes, Gilbert Phoenix, the actor who'd starred in many of Louis' favorite films. Louis was excited to get to see it on the big screen again inside a theater.

Jack was back in his office, watching Louis from his computer. Emily walked in with a fresh cup of hot coffee for the founder.

"Man, oh man…Emily."

"Yes, Mr. Jack?" she replied.

"People really love this nostalgia shit, huh?" he said as he watched Louis in virtual reality through the monitors.

"They most certainly do, Mr. Jack," she said before returning to the front desk.

When the level ended, Louis was proud of the day he had picked and his successful audition. Once he was back in real life, he felt a sense of accomplishment that he had not experienced since he was young. Like he'd achieved something important in his life.

Later that day, Louis said his goodbyes at the Mindtrick office building. On his way out, he saw Emily sitting at the front desk with a fresh cup of coffee. Just as she was about to take a drink, Louis ran over to her and knocked the cup out of her hand making it spill all over her desk.

"What the hell?" she said as a little bit of coffee got on her skirt.

"I'm sorry I had to do that. But you need to quit drinking this stuff. Now and forever. Trust me," said Louis.

"Trust you over Mr. Jack?" Emily asked.

"With this, yes. You'll thank me later."

Once he opened the front door and found himself outside on the street, it took only a few seconds for a random passerby to recognize him.

"You're Louis Parker!" said the man. He pulled out his cell phone and snapped a selfie with him.

"Yes, yes I am," Louis replied. He was quite confused. On his way to the car, more people recognized him. He had no clue what was going on, but he liked the attention.

Am I famous now? Louis asked himself.

On his ride home from work, he made a left onto the exit for Hazelberry. That is when he saw it. A humungous billboard on the side of the road with his picture and a bunch of people who looked to be in some sort of television sitcom called, "Following the Finklesteins."

"What in the world?" Louis asked himself as he drove by the large billboard with his own smiling face staring back at him.

When Louis returned home, he opened his laptop and did a web search on himself. Over twenty relatively well-known Hollywood movies and television shows came up in the results. Then he found a few movies with his face on the official poster. *Holy shit*, he said to himself He was taken aback.

Damn. I'm a god damned star!

After Louis got some sleep, he woke up and decided to test out his new life. He walked around the streets of San Diego, embracing any and all fans that spotted him. It felt great signing autographs and taking pictures. He never imagined himself doing anything like that sort of thing. He never got attention like that from anyone, let alone groups of people.

He was a little bummed that he did not get to live through the days he made the movies. Louis wondered what those experiences were like. What he missed out on. Those must have been some great moments for him. But for now, people knew who he was, which was a first for him. Even if it felt remarkably familiar to him in the back of his mind.

Later that day, Louis found himself at a strip club, drinking and mingling with the dancers who all had seen at least one of his films. They were adoring him like he was the most famous local celebrity around.

He soaked it all in. Everybody seemed to know him. Louis felt like he was a totally different person. Somebody people gave a damn about. He wondered what his movies were like. Were they good or bad, dramatic or cringe-worthy?

While he was leaving the club, Louis was surprised to find himself nearly trampled by paparazzi trying to snap his photo to evade them, Louis ran face-first into a telephone pole. "Dammit! Leave me alone," he yelled and ran away from the flashing cameras into the darkness of a nearby alleyway.

Later that week, Louis dined with some new Hollywood friends. He sat back in his chair and thought long and hard. His friends all chatted about their new gigs, and their latest hook-ups. Louis was zoning out, almost to the point of napping in the middle of dinner. He was bored. After not speaking for a few minutes, Louis sat up and said to his new friends, "What's the difference between a guitar and a tuna?"

The fellow actors turned their attention to Louis. One of them asked, "Tell us, Louie! What is it?"

"You can tune a guitar, but you can't tuna fish," said Louis.

After a moment of silence, everyone at the table started to laugh hysterically. It all felt so fake. Louis finally remembered his kids, and how they would never laugh at a corny joke like that. He got up from the table and walked out without explanation. One of his friends, child star Freddy Bastowksi, yelled out, "Louie! Where the hell you going? The night is just getting started!"

After a couple days of enjoying the actor life, he got bored of it all. He grew depressed when he remembered his kids and how much he missed them. Even after he rented all of the movies he was in and got to see how much of an impactful career he had in showbiz, all he wanted was his kids. He would do anything to go back to the way things were before he started working for Mindtrick games and testing *Seven Days VR*.

It was 1 p.m. when Louis walked out of the front door of his seven-bedroom mansion. This was the new home he found himself living in since he had become a successful Hollywood actor. He got into his rose-gold, self-driving Pulsar and headed to work.

Louis arrived at the Mindtrick Games building and parked on the sidewalk directly in front of the lobby. He stormed inside and made his way to Jack's office. Then, Louis kicked the door open and charged at his boss, knocking him out of his chair with a big left hook to the nose.

"What the hell?" said Jack as Louis punched him two more times, knocking the CEO off his balance and dropping him to the ground.

"That's for ruining my life," he said as he elbowed Jack twice in the jaw. "You won't get away with this," said Louis, and he walked out the door.

Jack slowly got back on his feet and followed his employee into the lobby. Everyone watched as Jack was bleeding from his nose. His eye began to swell as he followed Louis past the front desk in the lobby.

"You think your life has meaning?" asked Jack from a distance. Louis stopped by the front door and turned around.

"I know it does, asshole," Louis responded.

"I gave you a life, pal… You were an unemployed college dropout when I gave you the chance of a lifetime. Don't think I can't take this new successful life of fame and fortune away from you. Just like that!"

"You already took my life away, you sad, sad man."

Jack wiped away the blood from his nose as it kept gushing down his face. He walked over to Louis.

"I'm done here. I quit. Do your worst. I don't give a damn," said Louis.

"You're a dead man," said Jack.

"This one's for Cody." Louis cocked back and knocked Jack out with a spinning back fist to the jaw. Mr. Jack dropped to the floor.

"How's that for a reality check?" said Louis. "Lights out, Mr. Jack."

When security arrived, Louis had already left the building.

Chapter 20

Louis was getting gas for his Pulsar. At this point, Louis had enough money from TV and films that he no longer needed the job at Mindtrick. That was a good thing, considering he'd just punched out his boss.

He glanced around, left and right, to make sure he was not being followed by anyone, like Mindtrick security, or the police. A dark green car pulled up on the other side of the pump. Two girls in their mid-twenties recognized Louis.

"Oh…my…God!" yelled one of them. "Are you Louie Parker? From *Criminal Stockbroker*? And *Taste of Mud*?"

"I believe I very well might be. Sure."

"Oh boy, that's so lit. Like, we need a selfie! Elise! Get over here!" the driver yelled to her friend as she pulled out her cell phone. "I'm such a big fan, this is like, so crazy!" she yelled.

"Is it now?" asked Louis as he looked around hoping she was not bringing him too much unwanted attention. They came over and took a selfie with the movie star.

"Okay, I have to go, ladies," said Louis as he got in his car and drove off.

He checked his phone and saw the top-trending story on the social media app, MyFace: *Louis Parker wanted for assault.*

His phone rang as he turned onto Wallace Street and accelerated to nearly twice the speed limit. It was Jack who was calling, and Louis did not want to pick it up. Then he decided he was in too deep already, so he answered the call.

"What the hell do you want?" Louis said.

"Louie, nice right hook you got there. Knocked me out clean," said Jack.

"Yeah, well I'm starting to think I should have laid your ass out for good. You're a god damned lunatic. I should kill you, you bastard. You ruined my life!" yelled Louis as he switched lanes and sped past a dump truck.

"Look. I'm willing to call off the cops and put all this behind us, Louie," said Jack.

"You're nuts if you think I can trust you, Jack. You've taken everything from me!" said an emotional Louis.

"No! Just the opposite, Lou. I've given you another chance. Another life! Look at you, a freaking movie star. All the money you can ask for. Single, and a ladies' man. I've given you a fresh start. I could see it in your eyes. You were living a lie, Louie. And you made all these changes yourself. All I did was give you the key, but you opened the door…voluntarily. You finally found success."

"I lost my kids, you piece of crap. How can you sit there and think I would actually want that?" asked Louis bitterly.

"Lou, listen. I knew this was going to be an important mission, not just for you but for us. Obviously, mostly for us, but look at the understanding of self you have come to, my man," Jack explained. "You finally know who you are!"

"I want my old life back, dammit!" Louis cried.

"I'm sorry, bud, but you know that's not going to happen," said Jack. "Now, before you make things any worse, get your ass back here and let's settle this like grown-ups, shall we?"

"You're not going to get away with this. You're done," said Louis as he hung up the phone. He stomped on the gas pedal and went through a yellow light and around a church van. Then he grabbed a handful of cheezepuffs and stuffed his face as he put his car into self-driving mode and kicked his feet up for a moment. The rose-gold car made a sharp left turn onto Hamilton Avenue just before coming to a stop at a red light.

"Shit!" Louis yelled. *What the hell am I gonna do?* he asked himself in the mirror.

After driving for miles, looking everywhere to make sure he was not spotted by cops or fans, he got a call from Cody. The real Cody. Louis answered it.

"Cody, man. I'm freaking losing it. I don't know what the hell to do. I'm sure you've seen that the cops are looking for me by now," said Louis as he slowed down and turned onto a side street called Luna Road. The car was still in autopilot mode, so he did not have to focus on navigating.

"We don't have much time. Jack is going to have me slaughtered for this. Listen up. I'm going to text you an address to meet me at. I think I can help you get back to your old life, Louie," said Cody.

"I don't understand," said Louis.

"I don't doubt that. This is confusing shit. But if you do everything I say, we could reverse all of this. I think."

"How in the hell we gonna do that?" asked Louis.

"When I finished the algorithm for Version Two of Seven Days, I added a failsafe program. I coded a secret restart option that can only be used once. Listen, Jack doesn't even know about it. I noticed a long time ago the man can't be trusted, so I created it just in case anything got too crazy. Like a last resort of sorts. If we do this, Jack is going to have it out for me, he'll have me murdered right where I stand. But if all goes according to plan... he'll be behind bars for the rest of his damned life. But yeah, I'm fairly sure we can reverse everything," said Cody.

"How is that even possible?" asked Louis.

"It's called the "Day of Rest". It's quite simple. All you have to do is rest…or better yet, sleep. All day, on your Day Seven in the game. At that time, I'll initiate the shutdown protocol sequence which will let us trick the game into restarting. If we do that, the game will reset itself and it will go back to how life was for you when you began the trial of Version Two. It will be like nothing ever changed at all. In real life at least," Cody explained.

"If you're dead serious, then that's what we gotta do. What have I got to lose?" asked Louis. "I gotta do something, man. I miss my kids. I don't want to live in a world without them. I don't even care about any of the other shit. I don't need this fame. It ain't even for me, Cody. They need me. I need them."

"I understand, Louie. Okay, texting you right now. Will explain plans in more detail and give you further instructions when we meet. Talk soon," said Cody.

"Deal," said Louis before the call ended.

Louis got the text with the address in it. Then, he plugged it into his GPS on his phone and headed toward Cody's location. It was just under three miles from where he was. He put his smart car into hyperdrive and took off down the freeway. The car knew exactly where the lane lines were. Louis was nearly having a panic attack as his car drove him to the destination.

Louis arrived at a seedy warehouse, miles away from civilization. A bright neon yellow car whipped around the corner and pulled up next to him. It was Cody. "Get in," he said.

He got into the passenger seat just before Cody said, "Throw your phone out the window, just for safe keeping. Your license plate and your phone would be their best chance of tracking you."

Louis threw his phone out the window, smashing it on the ground as Cody took off.

Louis' car put itself into reverse and began to drive itself back to Louis' house.

"We don't have much time," said Cody as he swerved around the corner. "I'm going to explain exactly what we have to do, even if it all sounds impossible. Just trust me."

"I'm all ears, Cody. You're pretty much the only one I can trust at this point," said Louis.

"So, here's what I got. We need to steal the console and game beta and bring it to a motel outside of town. From there, you will have to play the last level of the trial. Like I said before. You can pick whatever day you want, and all you have to do is just sit there and relax, sleep, whatever. But you can't change a thing. You got that?" asked Cody as he reached into his car's center console and pulled out some beef jerky. He ripped it open and pulled out a piece. He offered Louis some which he declined. Cody took a big bite of the rough meat as he continued driving.

Louis started to speak. "So, what about..."

Cody interrupted. "I know what you're thinking. They're gonna see us sneaking in. Already got that covered. I'm going to call in a bomb threat, and we're going to use the secret back entrance door. After Jack fired me, I knew he would cancel all of my security clearances. So, I asked Jenna, who I used to date, if she could sneak me back into the system. She works in the HR department and she owed me a favor anyway."

"And once we got the game console and shit, we can do it all from a motel?" asked Louis.

"Yep. All we need is the console and the game. I can set it up to any monitor, or television, if need be. All that stuff at the lab is just fancy high-tech shiny furniture at the end of the day. All we need is the console and the game. And Wi-Fi of course," Cody continued. "Which this motel will have. If it's too slow, we can boost it from someone nearby. Whatever it takes."

Cody pulled up to a parking lot a few blocks from the Mindtrick Games corporate office.

"Here we go," he said as he pulled out his phone.

He blocked his number before calling the Mindtrick office. Emily picked up from the front desk. "Mindtrick Games. This is Emily."

With a different higher pitched voice Cody said, "Listen up. There is a bomb hidden in the lobby of your building, and it is going to go off in five minutes. This is no joke. If you don't evacuate the building, you will turn into ground beef, do you understand? The bomb will explode in less than five minutes. Tick tock, tick tock."

"This has to be a joke, right?" Emily responded.

"You tell me, Emily Friedman!" Cody said with a haunting voice through the other side of the phone.

"How do you know my last name?" Emily asked.

He then hung up and watched through the windows with binoculars. Moments later, dozens of people started evacuating the building. It worked just as they planned.

Cody and Louis got out of the car and hustled the two blocks to the Mindtrick offices.

They made it to the back door of the building. Cody took out his keycard and swiped it, as well as put his eye up against the scanner, opening the door. He was surprised it worked. "Nice, I can't believe Jenna actually came through for me. Now let's go, we don't have much time."

Then the two stealthily snuck around the offices until they got to the main lab where they did most of the testing. "We only have a couple of minutes until the bomb squad shows up," said Cody.

Cody grabbed all the headsets, wires, and controllers they would need. He made sure to snag all of the necessary plugs and chargers and stuffed them into his backpack.

Cody's phone started vibrating. He glanced at it, and then took the call. Louis looked out front and saw cops and bomb squad vehicles converging on the building.

"We gotta hurry!" Louis exclaimed.

Cody hung up the phone and looked over at Louis and said, "That was one of our coders, Andy. He's got more dirt on Jack. But come on. Help me carry this thing."

Cody started lifting the VR console.

"I gotcha," said Louis as he picked up the other side. They got out just in time before the bomb squad burst through the front doors with police officers behind them with guns drawn.

They reached Cody's car undetected, with the game disc and console in hand. They loaded it up in the trunk and drove off as quickly as they could.

While Louis drove, Cody called out the directions to the Lazy Lodge motel. Once Cody got all the information that he needed from his source, Andy, he got rid of his phone. Louis and Cody left their car at a gas station and took a taxi the rest of the way to the motel.

Thirty minutes later, they were checked into their motel room. This was where they planned to stay for the next two days. Cody had the virtual reality console set up with *Seven Days* installed and ready to go. Once Louis logged into the system and was connected entirely, he would be able to start where he left off at his last checkpoint which was the eve of Day Seven. But he started to feel some indecision. Perhaps his new life was, in fact, better than his old one. He had fame. Money. No more nagging ex-wife. No more financial troubles. Maybe this was the path that he was supposed to take originally. He was starting to second guess the whole plan entirely. He never got to experience the things the game had given him. But then, he remembered the only thing he missed, his kids.

"Screw it," said Louis. "Let's get this over with."

"All right," said Cody as he started to hook Louis up. He got him connected and as prepared as they could inside a shady motel in the middle of nowhere.

The game started, and the final level was ready to begin. "Here goes nothing," said Cody as he pushed "Start".

Louis was extracted into the virtual world instantly when Cody said, "Oh yeah, I forgot… What date are we going back to?"

Louis sat in the game's lobby and thought to himself, *does it even matter?*

"Let's go back ten years ago. I don't really care when."

"I got you," said Cody as he entered in the same day, ten years prior. "Blast off," he said as he hit "Enter".

Now that he had changed the ultimate outcomes with his previous levels, Louis wound up in a modest three-bedroom house on a third of an acre back in San Diego.

Then he remembered what Cody told him, and how the plan would only work if he rested and slept the entire time.

Louis had every urge in the world to get up out of bed. But instead he got comfortable and started to relax just like Cody instructed him to. He turned on his wireless home sound system, and played one of his favorite songs, "The Lizard People " by The Routers. He stayed in bed and tapped his chest to the beat of the drum. He hummed the melody of the chorus to himself as he drifted in and out of consciousness and began to nap.

Meanwhile, Cody was sitting on the motel bed, praying nobody would find them for the next day at least.

Then he opened his laptop and downloaded the files sent by his source, Andy. Once downloaded, Cody opened them and read through, astonished at the proof of Jack's crimes. Several documents included details of highly illegal black-market sales, including human trafficking, memory outsourcing, receipts of orders of Portomazine over the years, and connections to underground low-level terrorist leaders. Cody also learned of mass identity theft and other crimes against humanity. He composed an email to the local police and the FBI. He wrote it anonymously from a blocked proxy email address, but the evidence was clear and just enough to get Jack locked up for good.

He also attached the files he'd already hacked from Jack's laptop as additional proof of the crimes.

The email was sent.

All Cody had to do now was sit and wait patiently until Louis finished his final level in the game. He looked at the alarm clock and saw they had fifteen hours left. "This is gonna be a long day," Cody said to himself.

Time seemed to drag on forever in both reality and virtual reality. With all the temptation in the world, Louis stayed put and listened to music and watched his big screen TV in bed all day trying to kill time. He napped here and there but could not stay asleep as his mind continued to race.

When nighttime came, he finally passed out after finishing off a bottle of bourbon. Louis spent the rest of the simulation in Dreamland.

The "Day of Rest" program was complete, and the game shut off the moment the final level ended.

"Whoa," said Louis as he came to and ripped the VR headset off. He threw his controller gloves across the motel room. He was back to his original, lanky figure. He looked in the mirror and noticed he lost all the weight he had gained. He even craved a cigarette.

"Did it.... oh shit, did it really..."

"Work!?" yelled Cody as he ran over and hugged Louis. "I think it worked!"

Louis walked outside of the seedy motel. He saw a man in a white tank top smoking. Louis asked, "Hey, you got one I could bum?"

"Sure thing," said the man as he handed over a cigarette. The man lit up a lighter as Louis inhaled it in.

"Thanks," said Louis as he took a puff. "Damn, that's good."

Cody walked out of their room and said, "Welcome back to reality."

"Glad to be back," Louis responded as he took a drag of his cigarette. It reminded him of his first-time smoking, and it never felt so satisfying as it did at that very moment. Louis took one more drag before putting it out on the ground. He then ran back inside the motel room and picked up the landline phone on the table. He dialed his son's cell phone number.

Tommy answered, "Hello? Who's this?"

"Tommy! My boy! Is that really you?" asked Louis.

"Dad? Who the hell else would it be?" Tommy asked.

"You have no idea how glad I am to hear your voice, son."

"What? Dammit! Dad, you just made me die in my game, what is it? What's up? You could have just texted."

Louis began to cry and then said, "Oh, it's nothing. Nothing at all, son. Just wanted you to know that I love you."

"Dad, you're being weird," said Tommy. "But yeah okay, I love you too. Can I call you back in a little?"

Louis responded, "Yeah, sure, I just wanted to hear your voice.

"Right…" said Tommy.

"Listen how about you and your sister come over for dinner? I'll make burgers. I missed ya," said Louis as a tear dropped from his eye.

"Fine, Dad, anything so you let me get back to my game already," his son said.

Louis smiled. "Deal, I'll see you soon."

He hung up the phone and began to grin from ear to ear.

"Look at this, Louie," said Cody.

He turned his computer around to show a news headline that read: "Mindtrick Founder Busted on Multiple Felony Charges."

"No way!" said Louis as he read the article.

"Hopefully, justice is served, and that scumbag does a long time behind bars," said Cody.

"That's crazy, man. Good work," said Louis.

"Good work to you, too," Cody responded. "You did it, Louie."

They shook hands after they checked out of the motel. Before they left, Louis stopped him and asked if he could keep the console and give it to his son. Cody did not see a problem with it. The two called for taxis. They said their goodbyes and went their separate ways.

"It has been a pleasure knowing you, Cody," said Louis.

"The pleasure is all mine," said Cody.

Later that night, Louis was back at his apartment. He had asked his ex-wife Denise to bring the kids over because he did not have a car now as it was at the impound lot. He was no longer rich or famous, but he was happy. He still had some money saved up from the Mindtrick trials.

Denise pulled up in front of his building. The kids climbed out of the backseat and Louis never felt so happy to see them. He hugged them tightly. Days before, he did not know if he would see them ever again. They did not even exist.

Louis looked into the passenger window where his ex-wife's new boyfriend was sitting. She rolled down the window and Louis said, "Listen, Denise, I just want you to know, I'll always have love for you. You gave me the two greatest gifts in the world." He smiled at his kids. Then he looked at her new boyfriend and said, "You treat this woman well, you hear? She deserves the best."

Louis patted him on the shoulder. The man rolled his eyes.

Denise said, "What's gotten into you, Lou?"

"Guess I'm simply…well, I'm happy, you know? Life is…good. Really good," said Louis.

"Got it, Louie. Take good care of them. They really do love you, you know," said Denise.

Denise hesitated, as if she were about to say a lot more to her ex, but quickly realizing it might make her new boyfriend uncomfortable, she stopped herself.

"You were going to say something else?" asked Louis.

"No. Not really. Never mind. Just have a nice time together," Denise added.

Then, in a flash, she and her boyfriend drove off as Louis, Tommy, and Natalie went inside Louis' house.

At the dinner table, they were all eating cheeseburgers when Louis said, "So... I been thinking of getting a new job. Something...simple."

Tommy and Natalie did not respond as they were distracted by their smartphones, as usual. Louis was surprised, however, that this time, it did not seem to bother him as much as it used to.

He smiled and looked up to the ceiling fan and said, "Thank you. This is all I ever wanted. Thank you!"

After dinner, Louis sent a text to Jack's secretary, Emily. It was short and simply said, "Free for dinner Friday night?"

Within seconds, Emily replied, "Yes."

"Text me your address and I'll pick you up around seven," he wrote back.

Louis put his phone away and then he brought out a surprise gift for his son covered in wrapping paper. "This is for you, bud," he said to Tommy. "Early birthday gift."

"Holy shit!" his son yelled as he ripped off all of the wrapping paper to find the SB60 console that Cody gave to Louis.

"Watch your language," said Louis before laughing.

"This…is…awesome," said Tommy.

"Just a little gift from your pops," Louis said.

"I love it. Thank you so much. Wanna play the first game? Break it in?" his son asked.

Louis responded, "No thanks." He figured he had more than enough virtual reality to last him a lifetime. "But knock yourself out, son."

Tommy replied, "Suit yourself," as he immediately began to set up the system. He connected the cords to the back of the TV and plugged the SB60 into the wall.

"You know. One of these days I'll have to tell you about this game I tested at Mindtrick. Unfortunately, it won't be out any time soon if I were to guess."

"Oh yeah? You're crazy. That's crazy. What was the game called?" asked Tommy.

"*Seven Days in Virtual Reality*' or *Seven Days in VR*. It doesn't matter. It was pretty much nearly impossible to beat. But you know what? I did it. I beat it. With the help of one of my friends who used to work there. A coder named Cody. Your old man pulled it off," Louis said as he looked at his son and smiled.

Louis took a deep breath, as he continued, "Almost didn't think I'd beat it. If I didn't, things really would be different right now, son."

He took a long pause and then said, "Lemme tell you something, Tommy. There are so many events and outcomes in my life I wish I could change. Recently I figured out there are actually some events that I *can* change, even at my age. I just might go back to college. Or maybe I'll try to become an actor again. Did you know I once wanted to be an actor? What do you think of that? But I also realized there are some things about my life that I would not change. Yes, I am absolutely so proud and grateful that you and your sister are my children.

"Tommy, do I tell you often enough how much I love you and how pleased I am with you? Do I say that enough times to your sister? No game could ever take that away from me."

"You're not making any sense, Dad. Are you all right?"

"No worries. Let's just say that I beat a virtually unbeatable game."

"Cool, Dad. Sounds neat," Tommy said, sarcastically. "Now would you give me a hand with this? Help me figure it out. I have no clue how to set this thing up."

Louis responded, "Sure thing. But only if you promise me one thing. You'll go outside and play ball, ride your bicycle, take a walk, or do something like that from time to time. These games are fun here and there, but don't forget to live in the real world. Tommy, nothing beats real life. Don't forget that, son."

"Great speech, Dad. But I think at my age I'm thinking more about driving a car than riding a bike. But I get your point. So, now, can I please play? This looks awesome," his son responded.

"Right. Sorry. Go for it. Enjoy. Oh wait, I forgot. Let me take out the game that's in there now," he said before ejecting the *Seven Days VR* Version Two beta disc. Once the game ejected, Louis took it out and snapped the disc in half.

"Could you find one of those five games I bought you recently? Try one of those games instead. This one was defective."

About the Author

JEFF YAGER's published works include the YA novel *Atom & Eve* and *I Like God*, co-authored with Skye Bynes, a novel about social media. Inspired by his son Bradley, Jeff is the author of two children's books, *The Question is Why?* and *Chuck and Alfonzo,* about the friendship between a monkey and a dog. Nancy Batra is the illustrator.

He has an associate degree from Pasco-Hernandez State College. Jeff grew up in Stamford, Connecticut, relocating more than a decade ago to Florida, where he lives in a town outside of Tampa.

For more on Jeff, go to: https://jeffyager.us

Other works by Jeff Yager published by Hannacroix Creek Books, Inc.

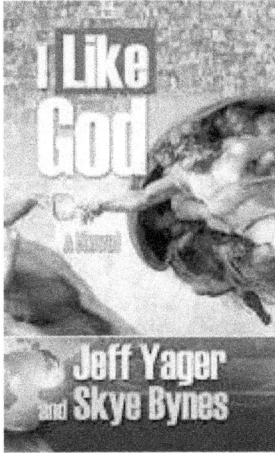

I Like God

A Novel

Jeff Yager and Skye Bynes

Joey Taylor jokingly starts a public page for "God" on FaceSpace and forgets about it when he goes off the grid from social media. Four years later, he returns to the page to find that it has over 30 million "likes." When Joey discovers the immense power and responsibility that comes with this incredible online audience at his disposal, the former pizza delivery driver develops a God complex of his own. Joey's newfound fame on FaceSpace takes a turn nobody could ever see coming.

Praise for *I LIKE GOD*:

I Like God: A Novel is one of those impressively written works of fiction that reveals something of what could really come to pass in today's social media dominated popular culture. A ripping great read from beginning to end, *I Like God: A Novel* is very highly recommended for community library General Fiction collections.... —Micah Andrew, Reviewer (Midwest Book Review)

My Lucky Hat
A Short Story
Jeff Yager
Available as an e-book with an audiobook version narrated and produced by Russell D. Bernstein

Have you ever had a piece of clothing, or an object, that you thought brought you luck? Keenan, a college student, finds the red hat that his Dad originally bought for him at a flea market when he was twelve. But can a hat really be lucky?

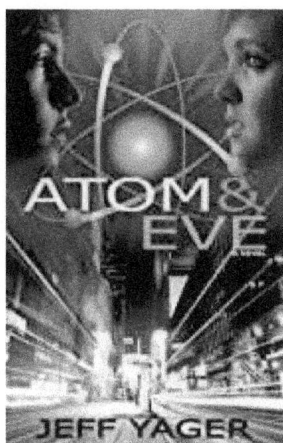

Atom & Eve

YA Novel

Jeff Yager

2013

Available in e-book, print, and audiobook versions.

They say truth is stranger than fiction and *Atom & Eve,* the prophetic novel about a deadly pandemic with no cure, is an example of that. In this sci-fi thriller, sixteen-year-old Ricky Romanello is a college freshman playing basketball when he collapses and winds up in a coma. He suffers from the powerful virus that hits the U.S. population causing deaths and a dramatic economic slowdown. As the virus quickly becomes a global pandemic, research scientist Dr. Mandy Fox has been developing an anti-aging drug that she believes might also eradicate the flu. Ricky takes the drug. But soon he, and everyone else who takes it, soon discover the new drug's unintended side effects. There is an intriguing subplot about the campaign of the first female candidate for

President of the United States. *Atom & Eve* was published when the author was just 23.

Praise for *ATOM & EVE*:

"...a great debut for its author, Jeff Yager. Its mix of suspense, science, romance, and even politics will keep the reader turning the pages to find out what happens next, and there are enough twists and turns to ensure the pace never slackens."—Alan Caruba, Editor, Bookviews.com, Founding member of the National Book Critics Circle

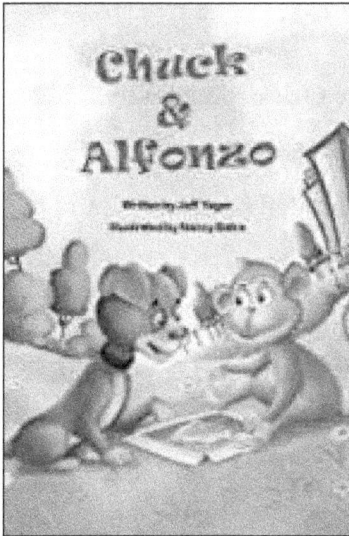

Chuck & Alfonzo

Written by Jeff Yager

Illustrated by Nancy Batra

Ages 5-8 2021

Chuck and Alfonzo is the story about an unexpected friendship that develops between a monkey named Alfonzo who escapes from the zoo and a dog named Chuck who runs away from Ryan, his owner. After a taste of freedom, will Chuck continue to explore the community on his own, or will he go back home?

Praise for *CHUCK AND ALFONZO*:

"*Chuck and Alfonzo* shows children that friendships can be created when least expected, no matter what their background is or where they come from. It also demonstrates how friends help each other when facing difficult decisions.—Emily Flint

"I like that two different kinds of animals became friends."—7-year-old Brianne

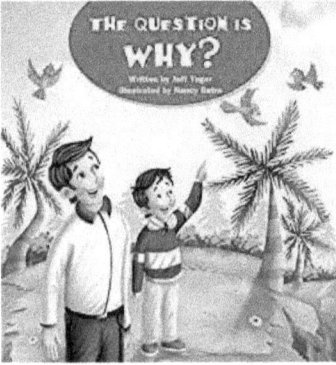

The Question is Why?
Written by Jeff Yager
Illustrated by Nancy Batra
Ages 2-6 2016
Available in e-book,
hardcover, and paperback

By a certain age, most children become very curious and they start asking "Why?" When a parent, teacher, or grandparent responds with an answer, these inquisitive children will often respond with another "Why?" *The Question is Why?* was inspired by the author's son, Bradley. In this fun and unique illustrated children's book, there are 26 different questions and answers, each corresponding to a letter of the alphabet. The book includes an illustrated alphabet chart, suggested books for further reading, and a list of fun activities.

Praise for *THE QUESTION IS WHY?*

"The Question is Why? incorporates both creative questioning AND an innovative take on learning the

alphabet. It will make a great addition to any Pre-K or K-3 classroom library!"—Kaitlin Roig-DeBellis, author, *Choosing Hope*; former first grade teacher, Sandy Hook Elementary School; and Executive Director, www.classes4classes.org

La Pregunta Es Por Que?
Jeff Yager
Ilustrado para Nancy Batra
Translated by Karen Raicher and Adriana de Almeida Navarro
2020

A los ninos les gusta preguntar "por que?" Esta encantador libro ilustrado para ninos tiene las respuestas, de la A a la Z.